GROUSE AND WOODCOCK

NICK SISLEY

GROUSE AND WOODCOCK

AN UPLAND HUNTER'S BOOK

Stackpole Books

Grouse and Woodcock: An Upland Hunter's Book
Copyright © 1980 by
Nick Sisley

Published by
STACKPOLE BOOKS
Cameron and Kelker Streets
P. O. Box 1831
Harrisburg, Pa. 17105

Published simultaneously in Don Mills, Ontario, Canada
by Thomas Nelson & Sons, Ltd.

Printed in the U.S.A.

Library of Congress Cataloging in Publication Data

Sisley, Nick.
  Grouse and Woodcock.

  Includes index.
  1. Grouse shooting. 2. Woodcock shooting.
I. Title.
SK325.G7S58   1979   799.2'48'61   79-15388
ISBN 0-8117-0717-2

Contents

This book is dedicated to Roger Latham, close friend and former outdoor editor of the *Pittsburgh Press*. Rog was one of the best outdoor writers of all time. He fell to his death while photographing ibex and chamois in Switzerland a few months prior to the publication of this book. Though Rog loved all facets of the outdoors he was first and foremost a grouse and woodcock hunter.

Introduction

When I sold my first magazine story back in 1966, it was about a woodcock hunting experience. That first sale launched me on a writing career from which there was no turning back. Regardless of the successes and failures of the intervening years, it has been my love of grouse and woodcock hunting, dogs, and shooting that got me into this business, and these are the reasons I stay in it. For better or for worse, these subjects comprise what the world is all about for me.

In each chapter I have attempted to choose a personal hunting experience to illustrate my point. Although this anecdotal approach isn't new to the outdoor writing field, it is one that is seen less and less in the outdoor magazines. My attempt has been to present suggestions for increasing knowledge and hunting skills with grouse and woodcock in a form that will be readable and entertaining. The chapters alternate back and forth between the two birds, with grouse always getting top billing, and woodcock coming up second. Any chapter can be read last, first, or in the middle, and it will not break the continuity.

The main purpose of this book has been to entertain. I don't pretend to be the world's best bird hunter, the country's finest wingshot, or to know more about upland habitat than anyone else. I wrote this book because grouse and woodcock are what I love most. Besides entertaining, I hope this book will make readers more efficient hunters of these two birds. I hope I've also planted a seed of conservation that readers will respond to by supporting The Ruffed Grouse Society, knowledgeable game managers, and grouse and woodcock research.

1

All About Grouse

Long before official sunup each spring day, the male grouse leaves his nighttime bedding spot. As the first rays of light send faint beams of brightness over the eastern horizon, the bird takes his early morning stroll. He heads for his favorite drumming log.

He approaches the drumming site warily. He knows he's going to be vulnerable once his performance starts, so he cautiously checks for danger before beginning. His head darts up and down and from side to side—odd-looking antics. Then he hops up on his log perch and goes through more head bobs. He paces back and forth on his log before getting down to business.

His magnificent tail fans out to display every feather fully. Up come the shiny black hackles on his ruffed neck until they're sticking out almost straight. He maintains that attitude for several steps, making a few circles. Then his tail settles down tight against the log, giving him a firmer base from which to hold his body still while his wings begin their drumming role.

The drumming almost invariably starts with one beat, but his call to the lovelorn is quickly followed by another, then another. The cadence changes from single drums to a roll so fast it would put the great Gene Krupa to shame. The sound is produced as the wings create a vacuum. The air rushing in to fill the void causes the noise.

Drumming male grouse.

No eye can keep the wings in focus—they move so fast. After the first drumming roll, which might last five to ten seconds, the cock grouse will strut back and forth on his perch, hoping to glimpse an amorous female who might have been attracted to his performance. He also checks closely for a male who might be challenging his territorial rights. He won't rest long. Soon he feels the need to go through this spring drumming ritual again. Down goes his fanned tail against the perch, out pop his neck ruffs, out stretch his wings. A thump resounds, followed by faster and faster thumps until the individual sounds are lost in the roar of the drumming roll.

While males are known to drum every month of the year, spring is when they can be depended upon to perform several times a day. Trout fishermen often hear this drummer of the woods while they're casting a favorite pool. Spring turkey hunters can be similarly entertained if they're in the right spot at the right time. But, grouse hunters might dabble in the sport for years and never hear a bird drumming during hunting season. Many ruff buffs are so interested in their favorite bird, however, that they take special pains to locate drumming logs, then return in the spring to witness the spectacle in person, perhaps even to record the display with a camera. It's worth crawling out of bed early to observe the male's spring antics.

If you hear a grouse drumming in the fall, try to flush that bird. I've found that drumming grouse are so wary in October and November that I've never even had a shot at one, let alone bagged one I was trying to flush. But when you know their vicinity, it's easier to spot their perch. Often it's a fallen log, sometimes a large one; but in some cases the drumming perch might be a fairly small log, elevated ten to twenty inches off the ground. The key is the bird's droppings which he always leaves where he drums. It's possible to find a drumming log like this while hunting in the fall, or while dog training in late summer or early spring. Make a careful mental or written note of the sight.

To record the display with a camera, set up a blind as soon as possible. I recommend the green, flexible cloth that cemeteries use to line graves during funerals. This material can be draped over a light wood frame. Most will want a telephoto lens to photograph the drumming grouse. Be certain to check the shortest distance on which the lens will focus. Then put your blind two or three feet further back so that you'll have more depth of field opportunity. I suggest a 200mm telephoto as minimum, a 300mm lens maximum, but be certain it focuses close. Use a tripod and shutter release because most photo opportunities of drummers will be in low light situations, requiring open lens settings and slow shutter speeds.

Once the spring drumming starts it's important to be in your blind before the grouse gets up. Trying to sneak through the woods while he's performing will only result in spooking the bird for the day. Do it often enough and he may be spooked for good.

While grouse typically use logs for their drumming perches, they might use any elevated area—a stump, a mound, an upturned root, a large rock, etc. Old logs are definitely favored, seldom freshly cut ones. One of fair diameter and half-rotten with age is most typical. Some of these mossy covered logs are used by several generations of males.

Habitat

A drumming site is chosen with many factors in mind. The male's spring perch must be surrounded by good grouse habitat. This includes areas where the female can make the nest and incubate her eggs, areas where the newborn chicks can feast on a high protein diet of insects during the first weeks of warm weather, and areas of heavy cover where birds of any age can seek refuge from weather or predators.

The drumming site itself has specific requirements. It should offer the drumming grouse some protection from predators that fly overhead. This means a reasonably thick spot. But the drumming site can't be too thick, lest it be ideal for a fox to lurk in the shadows a few feet from the log. Under these conditions a fox could nab a grouse in the middle of his drumming roll.

Grouse biologists are still trying to determine all the drumming site necessities and the surrounding habitat ingredients. Some biologists feel that the drumming site could be extremely important as a management tool that might permit us to promote a significant increase in the number of fall grouse. First we must learn more about what ingredients make up a great drumming site, then perhaps we can learn to reproduce these conditions, even if artificially.

The 1970s were typified, as far as grouse hunters were concerned, by great strides in grouse management through Gordon Gullion's toils with aspen as it relates to grouse habitat. No single management tool before or since has captured the imagination and the intellect of grouse hunters and grouse biologists like management of aspen. It continues to grow in importance as we swing into the 1980s, even though Gullion started his work back in the 1960s. If ever game managers have found the perfect habitat to manage for grouse, it's aspen. As much as we've all learned during the last decade, we're continuing to learn more, and the prospects for aspen management seem to look even brighter than ever.

Before this research work started, aspen had no commercial use. Although a hard wood, loggers disdained aspen, called it a weed, and left it on recently cut forest floors. But during a paper crunch, pulp mills were forced to learn how to use aspen in paper making because nothing else was available. Once they learned aspen could be used in the making of some low grade papers like newsprint and a few others, they used it more and more. It was readily available and cheap.

Then a Canadian manufacturer of wood products saw how much aspen was left in the woods and how quickly aspen replenished itself when clones were cut. They experimented by chipping the aspen with special saws or knives, then gluing the pieces back together with modern super-strength adhesives. The resultant glued chips, rolled and pressed into cut lengths, is the product known today under several trade names, probably the most popular being Aspenite. Used as a replacement for plywood (which has grown extremely expensive) and other wood products, glued and pressed aspen chips are becoming especially popular with the construction industry. Mills that produce this new board are capable of high volume, requiring enough aspen to create a new grouse cover virtually every operating day.

The latest uses of aspen are even more promising, particularly for grouse hunters. More than one industry has already abandoned such fuels as natural gas, diesel, electricity, coal, and others because of escalating cost. They have converted to burning plentiful aspen to power their factories. It could be that in the not too distant future a few electric generating facilities will switch to aspen as their sole source of fuel. When they do, we'll have lower fuel bills and more grouse to hunt in October. And we can enjoy a sustained yield of continually produced fuel for a generating plant once it becomes sensible to switch to aspen as the fuel source. Wood fuels are continually replenishing themselves, unlike coal, natural gas, and oil. In many areas of the country aspen production is so reliable that a new crop is ready for cutting before the generating plant has used up its current available supply.

What is so special about aspen that makes it ideal for grouse? First it must be emphasized that aspen in one stage of maturity is lousy for grouse. Aspen in four different stages of maturity is required to provide habitat capable of producing large numbers of ruffs. Remember, however, even when perfect habitat is provided, there will be years when grouse numbers are down. Frankly, no one has figured out why populations of these birds fluctuate even when top habitat is available.

Grouse like maturing aspen trees in winter because they hop up on the limbs and eat the buds. This food is high in protein and it's available no matter how deep or crusted the snow might be. Grouse might eat aspen buds at any time of the year, but this food is especially beneficial during the height of the winter. Grouse also need thick escape cover in winter to find shelter from harsh elements and predators. When leaves are

Hunter working through young aspen cover.

gone from the trees, grouse can be an easy mark for a hawk. Maturing aspen is open, so it doesn't provide thick winter cover. Thickets are required at other times of the year, too.

The importance of drumming sites has already been covered. Cutting the forest leaves some logs in the form of slash from which the males can stake out their territory and lure in a mate. The freshly cut aspen patch, one that's had only a growing season or two, provides the thick escape cover. Females tend to make their nest close to, but not in, the openings created by aspen cutting. The young chicks look for the high protein insects along the edges of the openings shortly after they emerge from the nest. Insects are critical to a young grouse's well being. If the chicks can't get insects, and a lot of them, during the first two to six weeks of life, the young get a poor start. If they don't die early, they're seldom robust, falling prey to a number of diseases during the summer, or becoming easy marks for predators.

The crux of Gullion's work with grouse was finding that landowners and state or federal foresters could cut aspen on a rotation basis, and by doing so create ideal habitat conditions for grouse. The basic idea is to break down the management unit into quarters. So far it is believed that these managements units should be relatively small, perhaps twenty to one hundred fifty acres.

For illustrative purposes, let's assume the management plot measures forty acres. This plot is broken down into quarters, ten acres each. One ten-acre tract is cut immediately. Ten years after the first ten acres were cut, the second ten-acre quarter is harvested. Ten years later the third ten-acre quarter is harvested. Ten years later the fourth ten-acre quarter is harvested. Ten years after that, the plot cut first is ready for the chain saw again. Some foresters believe that aspen might be harvested even sooner than forty years. Naturally, growing season, soil fertility, rainfall, and many other factors come into play.

With this harvesting policy private landowners can enjoy

a continuing financial yield from their land while producing optimal grouse habitat. The state forester and federal forester can be doing the same thing on publicly-owned land. By separating the forest to be harvested into quarters, grouse are provided with mature timber, maturing timber, freshly cut areas, plus the in-between stage.

If this type of management is done on a large scale, from what we know now, it would not be advisable to clearcut large tracts. Forty-acre clearcuts appear near optimum for the present. Extremely small clearcuts are not attractive to the timberman, probably not to grouse, either. When an area intended for aspen management, separated in four units, is first harvested, there will probably be an intermixture of tree species felled. In areas like Wisconsin and Michigan, plus large parts of Minnesota, New York, Pennsylvania, and Ohio, aspen will be the primary species to regenerate—a bonus to the grouse of those states.

Another beautiful aspect of aspen is that it regenerates so well. No replanting or reseeding is necessary. When a tract is cut, new aspen stems shoot up from the root suckers of the old ones. Discing the soil after timbering permits even more root suckers to generate, but even this inexpensive management technique isn't essential. However, in some areas aspen doesn't grow at all, and in others aspen is a borderline species—in competition with other trees that might be better suited to the area. Aspen isn't the grouse cure-all for every state.

In my home state of Pennsylvania, the Game Commission has instigated several ambitious grouse habitat research projects. An especially interesting one is in the central part of the state where a study involves well over 100 ten-acre plots. Divided into quarters, these will be harvested 2½ acres at a time. Three different habitat types will be studied: primarily aspen, primarily scrub oak, and primarily mixed hardwoods. Longer cutting rotations for the mixed hardwoods are envisioned— perhaps an eighty-year rotation, cutting each quarter every twenty years. However, since many of these hardwoods are already in the forty- to fifty-year class, the first cutting sequence might be cut in half. An adjoining fifteen hundred acres, where no cutting will be done, will act as the control area. Flush rates, drumming grouse, and other factors that tell biologists about grouse numbers will be constantly monitored.

The impetus behind this study is to research various timber-cutting methods to see if any of them favor significant increases in grouse populations. It is much too early for any determinations or conclusions, but by the mid 1980s, I'm optimistic that we might have a great deal of beneficial knowledge gathered about timber management that can benefit the grouse population and other species of wildlife, too.

The grouse hunter must not forget that game biologists can't create high game populations and keep them there. They can only learn more and more about habitat conditions, work to provide habitat that they know is essential to high populations, then sit back and pray. It's an art that they try to put more science into with each passing season, but there are still large fluctuations in game levels.

Minnesota had tremendous increases in grouse levels in the late 1960s, and some of this must be attributed to Gullion's work and the increased harvest of aspen. However, while aspen habitat conditions were still improving in the early 1970s, grouse levels dropped off. Some were quick to claim we'd jumped to too many hopeful conclusions with respect to aspen and grouse. But the birds have made a comeback in Minnesota recently. I'm told in some areas of the state the hunting is even better than it was in the late 1960s. Learn to expect population changes, but also be willing to back knowledgeable biologists who are developing management practices that work, even if they don't work immediately.

What current-day grouse hunter hasn't dreamed about hunting in the days of yesteryear when a large part of the fall income could be derived from hunting grouse for the market? When man first arrived in America from Europe, it's my guess there were fewer grouse than there are today. But when the land was cleared for crops, the new openings created were ideal for broods. Then came the virtual devastation of almost every stick of timber, which took years to accomplish with the crude sawing methods utilized and the frontier-type shipping that was employed. Wildfires followed the timbering, preventing the reforestation process. In much of Appalachia, New England, and the upper Midwest, habitat conditions were ideal for grouse, and these conditions existed over literally millions of acres. No wonder there were so many birds for market hunters to harvest. No wonder daily game bags were so high. No wonder a market hunter and his dogs could develop such skill. They had a seemingly unending supply of birds to practice on.

Market hunters, no matter how monumental their bags, had nothing to do with the reduction in yesteryear's grouse supply. In the first place there were never that many market hunters willing to take on the hard life. More money could be made in industry or private business. It was the changing habitat that changed grouse hunting, making the bird a mark for sportsmen rather than a bird that could be harvested in tremendous numbers by experts. The wild fires were finally controlled or perhaps there wasn't any more slash to burn. The regenerating forest took over.

Grouse numbers remained relatively high until those regenerating forests reached a height that was too mature to be ideal for the ruffed grouse. Grouse numbers have been dwindling ever since. It has only been in recent years that once devastated forests have come back to the point where serious harvest on larger and larger scales has become a reality. It is only in these areas that ruffed grouse exist in good numbers, and flush rates of four or more birds per hour are possible.

Minnesota, Wisconsin, and Michigan are three states that are producing outstanding grouse hunting almost every fall, although all top spots will have their down years. States like New York, Pennsylvania, Ohio, and all of New England will probably enjoy better hunting in the 1980s than they did in the 1970s, if timber cutting continues, and if aspen and other woods are utilized on an escalating basis by commercial interests.

Current timber practices in the South do not favor this

Three grouse and a side-by-side double.

great bird. If they change, grouse hunters will benefit. Much of the cutting in the southern mountains is oriented toward selective harvest of mature trees. Such yields of timber don't do anything for grouse, and do little for most other wildlife species.

I am not aware of any studies that have shown any increase in grouse hunting activity, though such studies may exist. From my own experience I believe grouse hunters are definitely on the increase. Just how much they're increasing may be a question for game managers to probe. I'm convinced that hunting has no effect on the overall number of grouse, but I'm just as convinced that heavy pressure does make harvesting the grouse that remain almost impossible. They become so wary if pursued relentlessly that they flush farther and farther from the hunter and his dogs.

Physical Characteristics

Once the bird is in the bag, grouse hunters universally hold the bird in reverence, inspecting it with a long, loving look. It's during these inspections that the hunter tries to determine whether he has bagged a male or a female. Males tend to be slightly larger than females, especially mature males (those older than one-half year). Tail feathers are commonly what every hunter checks first. The long ones are said to belong to the males, the shorter ones to females; but length of tail feathers can be confusing. Even a biologist can't look at tail feathers and be certain of sex 100 percent of the time.

Whether or not the band in the fantail is broken in the middle is said to be another key. The unbroken bands are those of the males. I have particularly poor luck looking at a tail band and guessing sex, although a certain percentage are obvious.

The neck ruffs are another sex indicator. The larger, more iridescent, more prominent ruffs are said to belong to the males. Again, the degree of subjectivity is great. A few stand out like sore thumbs as being males. The majority make me shake my head in wonder.

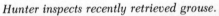

Hunter inspects recently retrieved grouse.

John Kriz, one of the most knowledgeable grouse biologists I've ever had the pleasure of sharing cover and experience with, showed me a system that is almost 100 percent foolproof. He checks the rump feathers just up from the tail. Those with one dot are male, two white dots female. I've studied his work, then studied those small white flecks on those rump feathers, and have been only occasionally confused.

Andy Ammann, retired grouse biologist from Michigan, showed me a foolproof way of determining the sex of grouse that's so easy I'm surprised I've never seen it mentioned in print, and no biologist I've talked with knows about it. Males have a prominent slash of bright orange above the eye. (See photo.) Raise the feathers above the eye with a finger or thumb. If the bird is a male, the orange mark will be readily apparent. If it's not there, the bird is a female. I say this method is foolproof because I've been able to accurately determine the sex of every grouse I've handled in the last four years by checking above the eye. Statistically, grouse biologists might want to check many hundreds of birds before they say it's foolproof. Of course, the ultimate gender check comes after removing the entrails so the bird's body cavity can be checked to determine whether an egg sack or gonads are present.

The ruffed grouse's scientific name is *Bonasa umbellus*. A gallinaceous bird, it has a heavy body, stubby wings, legs adapted to running and scratching for food, and a crop into which food is swallowed to be digested later in a powerful stomach muscle, with some type of grit or grinding compound mixed with the food being crunched.

Nesting takes place in late spring. This will vary with latitude, late May being the average month for brood hatching. As a ground nester capable of large broods, the grouse usually produces ten to fourteen eggs per nest. During incubation, cold rains can devastate them all. The female may nest again, but grouse hunters hope for reasonably dry springs. Cold rains shortly after the grouse are hatched can also be devastating to

Male grouse have a bright orange spot above their eye.

the fall flock. Not only can the dampness and the chill actually kill the young, the lack of sun will result in fewer insects which are necessary for a chick's good start in life.

The brood stays with their mother all through the summer, even into the early fall. Seemingly, they learn from her about how to forage and to be wary of intruders to their domain. At some time in the fall the brood begins to break up. It seldom happens all at once. In the early season, many hunters encounter multiple flushes if they're working good cover. Usually this means they've encountered a brood, some of which may have already left the flock.

This fall breakup is nature's way of scattering the family for the cold months when they are most vulnerable. Having them leave the cover of their birth also gives nature a chance to populate areas where there may be fewer birds, although ideal habitat is always a necessary ingredient. It's doubtful that a young grouse travels very far, if in fact it does try to inhabit a new cover.

The phenomenon "crazy flight" is often attributed to this fall breakup. It's usually in the fall that grouse fly into windows of rural homes. Maybe these birds go a little berserk from living in such close proximity to their brothers and sisters all summer long. When they get fed up they might depart in a hysterical manner, intending to leave their brethren forever, only to meet their demise on a window pane. Some claim that reflection of their own image is a factor in such deaths, but I tend to think these grouse must be trying to fly through what they think is an opening (the glass). Though an interesting phenomenon from which countless speculations can be drawn, crazy flight doesn't kill very many birds.

The ruffed grouse is the most challenging target in all huntingdom. Occasionally an easy mark, grouse are more typically found in cover where quick shots at a blurry brown buzz bomb disappearing into the foliage are the rule, not the exception. No sport requires faster gun handling. No hunting requires the sportsman to be more constantly attentive. No bird is tougher for a dog to handle in impeccable fashion than a grouse whose forefathers have been pursued by a legion of scattergun-toting woodsmen. No bird puts an obstacle between himself and the shotgun muzzle as consistently as the grouse. No small game animal brings a broader smile of contentment to the hunter's face and soul than a freshly retrieved, plump, warm ruffed grouse.

2

All About Woodcock

It had been a cloudy afternoon, and the sun dropped off the western horizon unseen. The clouds turned a darker gray. I heaved a shoulder against a creek bottom sycamore. The dog, tired after a period of spring training, seemed glad to sit quietly on her haunches at my side, panting softly, looking at me anxiously. I hadn't heard or seen the mating flight for a year now, but I knew a woodcock or two would put on an aerial display tonight, for the dog and I had flushed several during our training session. Still, darkness was making a rapid onset and nothing was happening.

I strained my ears, listening for any telltale sound. They might be working a nearby singing field instead of the one I was watching. Then I heard the first indication, a loud "peent," guttural and loud enough to be heard for quite a distance, although this one was relatively close at hand. Less than a minute later the long-billed woodcock uttered his deep, chesty call again, then several more times before he finally launched into flight.

In the twilight they're not easy to see, even if the anxious observer is standing relatively close. But I saw that male helicopter up from his pad. He made a wide circle without gaining much altitude; the whole time his outer primaries were singing that liquid twitter so easily recognized in October when this bird jumps in front of the pointing dog as the hunter walks in. Biologists are positive the outer primaries are the cause of the noisy twitter. They've trapped woodcock live during banding sessions, pulled the outer primaries, and helped the birds fly by using their hands as a launch pad. No sound results after such feather removal.

This male circled, gaining altitude slowly at first, but then his circles grew smaller as he flew higher. I squinted, trying to watch him ascend for as long as possible. Finally he disappeared from view, but his wing song continued. After he disappeared for several seconds the wing twitter ceased. The silence lasted only briefly. As the woodcock's descent began, he turned on his vocal cords. The sound was not unlike his wing twitter, though it was definitely different, even more liquid in nature, a softer song. In view again, still high, the woodcock descended so fast it was difficult for the eye to keep up. His warbling continued, getting louder as he came closer. Fifty feet above the ground he stopped his singing, spread his wings and tail to slow for landing, then touched down not far from where he'd launched, as softly as a dropped cottonball. Seconds later he reached deep into his vocal chords, maybe even into his chest, for a low and even more guttural "peent!"

The dog at my side had heard the display. She was sitting with ears perked, ready to dash off for another hunting stint, even if night was drawing near. But she looked up at me, saw my stern face meant for her to stay, and she seemed content, panting less forcefully now. By the time I looked back up, the woodcock was again trying to impress any impressionable

female that might be within hearing with another loud "peent."
Several more calls were uttered at regular intervals, then the
bird made a second flight almost an exact duplicate of the first.

The dog and I stayed until the very end, when the wing
twitters, the guttural "peents," and the marvelously liquid singing had ceased for another day. It appeared our star performer
had not attracted a mate that session. Maybe tomorrow morning he would have better luck. I told the dog to heel and we
eased back to the pickup. Though I take time every spring to
view this phenomenon, the mating flight of the male woodcock never ceases to thrill me to my marrow.

While the primary purpose of the courting flight is to
attract and impress a female, an almost equally important
purpose is the male's staking out his parcel of real estate, the
territorial imperative. His "peents," his flight, his wing twitters,
and his liquid song are also a warning that intruding males
will get punched in the nose. Often more than one male can be
heard "peenting" in the same area, but their flights won't be as
often, if at all, compared to the dominant male. These guys
know their place on the pecking order. They won't move up
until the following spring, or until they find their own singing
field.

A singing field is an opening in the surrounding forest, a
place where a male can more effectively stake out his claim, a
place where the female being courted can better see her lover.
Any old forest opening won't do. It is essential that nesting
cover be close by, preferably less than a couple of hundred
yards away. Brood cover, always lower, younger, thicker stuff
is yet another essential. Worms, the birds' lifeline, must be
available in reasonably protected cover, too. Undoubtedly
there are some other habitat essentials. The fact is that productive singing fields are few and far between.

It's an almost sure-fire bet that singing fields exist in or
near your favorite woodcock cover, however. While habitat
changes may occur as the seasons change, fall cover does have
similarities to spring cover. I continually find woodcock males

providing exciting flight antics in the spring where I've shot woodcock the previous fall.

Physical Characteristics

The woodcock is a transplant. Once a shore bird, maybe a lot like the jacksnipe, woodcock cruised and fed on the shores of lakes, marshes, and the ocean. Why woodcock gave up on this type of habitat in exchange for an upland life, I won't speculate.

Woodcock on the ground.

The woodcock is scientifically interesting because it's so different. The long bill is the first bit of originality to catch the observer's eye. The woodcock uses that bill to probe into the ground, usually for earthworms (of which there are numerous different species), but sometimes for grubs, larvae, or other high protein insect life. The next time you kill a woodcock, look closely at that bill. Note that it is rigid its full length, but flexible at the very tip—most unusual. Its purpose is to enable the bird to pierce the soft, moist ground with a closed bill, yet open the very tip when that long bill is buried, grasp the worm firmly, then pull it topside where it'll gulp it like a robin.

You'll have to look more closely to find the woodcock's ears, another anomaly. They're situated toward the front of the head rather than below or behind the bug eyes. Nature's purpose? Let's postulate that the woodcock uses its hearing to listen for subtle earthworm movements underground. Picture the bird standing at a boggy place in your favorite cover. It will spend a great deal of time posed silently, maybe take a few steps, seemingly listening intently again. Then suddenly the woodcock will stab its bill deep into the ground, bringing up a worm. If those ears were set farther back, how could the bird hear those underground worm movements?

After the long bill, the woodcock's next most prominent feature is its eye. Why is it so big? And they're not forward on the face, they're more toward the sides and rear. Seemingly the woodcock can look behind and above better than forward or down. Most assume the woodcock's eyes are large because of nocturnal habits. With greater light gathering power, the woodcock is better equipped to feed at night and at dusk, to perform (or watch) the mating flight in minimal light, to migrate at night, etc.

Biologists have found that there's a definite correlation between light intensity of a cover and flush rate. More woodcock are found in thick, low light covers on sunny days, in slightly more open, higher light covers on cloudy days. Maybe this is a result of the great light gathering ability of their eyes;

perhaps they can't stand too much brightness. With the eyes set back atop the head, the bird can still look around for danger when its bill is poked underground. Although it's doubtful a flying predator would zoom down through thick alders or aspen tangles to snatch up a feeding woodcock, these birds do move into more open terrain to feed under cover of waning light. Several flying predators are active then.

As the woodcock's eyes have moved backward on its head over the eons of evolution, the bird's brain has been displaced, too. The result is a brain that is now literally upside down. No wonder his flush antics in front of a pointing dog can be so unpredictable!

To the not-so-casual observer, the third most obvious unusual characteristic of this bird, after its bill and eyes, is the bird's heart. It's huge. So is the bird's liver. I wonder if both don't help the woodcock be more hardy, helping the bird to stave off fatigue and starvation during long stints without food, such as during migration and/or when the bird is caught in a freeze and can't probe.

There's little or no color difference between a male and a female woodcock, but there's a significant size difference. The female is bigger. There are several other ways biologists differentiate between the sexes. The hunter can learn to do it himself with only a little training. The three longest feathers on the leading edge of the wing (outer primaries) are rather thin in the male, wider in females. Bills that are under sixty-three millimeters belong to males; those that measure longer than seventy-two millimeters belong to females. Those that measure between can be either. Check the primaries. It's well to also note that females comprise 95 percent of those with bills seventy to seventy-two millimeters, and that the same percentage applies to males with bills measuring sixty-four to sixty-six millimeters.

I still occasionally hear experienced woodcock hunters claim that native woodcock are big birds, flight woodcock are smaller. Such claims are heard less and less these days because

Hunter inspects the outer primaries of a woodcock. The outer primaries are used to determine sex, and these feathers create the woodcock's "twittering" flight sound.

scientists have proven the females are bigger, and that fact has appeared in print many times. A hunter only displays his lack of woodcock knowledge when he makes claims to the contrary.

It's rather easy for scientists to trap live woodcock in the spring. Fresh from the long migration flight from the wintering grounds, males tend to weigh between 125 and 130 grams, females weigh between 165 and 170 grams. When hatched, the little chicks may weigh less than 15 grams.

Lawrence Cignetti and I were scouring a favorite fall cover one March. It was the last day of the month, when dog training season ends in my home state. We had enjoyed several points that afternoon, which was cloudy, damp, and cool. One of the dogs locked on point along an edge, then the bird flushed while Lawrence and I were walking in. But it was such an unusual departure the dog broke. No wonder! The woodcock, a fat female, was twittering this way and that, almost landing, then taking back off again just as the dog raced in close. She lured him one hundred yards off before taking wing in seemingly perfect flight, making a wide circle.

I knew immediately that a brood must be on the ground. Since I had never seen a recently emerged chick, I had to take a look. I almost tramped on one before I spotted the quartet. By dumb luck I had the camera around my neck, so I put a chick in my palm, took a few pictures in the dim light, then put the bird back down. Lawrence and I hurried away from the vicinity, hoping we hadn't done any harm and that the mother would come back to her young soon. It was unusual that she had her brood in fairly open terrain, for woodcock females usually take their young chicks to much thicker cover as soon as they emerge from the nest. A nest typically has four eggs.

During spring dog training sessions I've found a number of woodcock nests. These birds must be exceptionally hardy to nest before the end of March in Pennsylvania. I recall finding one nest on February 24, by far the earliest date. The birds haven't even returned that early in recent years, let alone set up homekeeping. Two of the nests I've discovered in March didn't hatch young. Both were located on flood plain habitat. When heavy rains came the engineers controlling the gates at the dam had to back the water up to prevent downstream flooding. Those nests were covered with water before the incubation period was completed.

Two woodcock chicks hours after hatching.

Hunters are accustomed to finding woodcock in essentially the same habitat fall after fall, so most of them don't realize that there are subtle changes in habitat requirements from summer to fall and from daytime to nighttime. Woodcock tend to spend daylight hours in relatively heavy cover (diurnal habitat), then fly to more open fields to feed at dusk or at night (nocturnal habitat). This is especially true in the summer, and into the early fall. The term "dusking woodcock" originates from illegal shooting that takes place during these late flights, which are invariably after sunset.

During the spring return to the nesting grounds, the males are always the first to arrive. While they don't choose the nest site, they do choose the general area for the female since all nests are within a couple of hundred yards of a singing field. By netting banded woodcock in the spring, biologists have proven that the same males and females keep returning to the same singing grounds every year. The homing instinct is obviously very strong.

Habitat

Generally speaking, woodcock nest north of the Mason-Dixon Line. Some nesting takes place in the mountains of West Virginia, Virginia, and Maryland, some on the Delmarva Peninsula, but more brood rearing, by far, takes place farther north. The Canadian provinces of Ontario, Quebec, and New Brunswick nest large numbers of woodcock, while Nova Scotia and Prince Edward Island harbor fair numbers, too. The states of Michigan, New York, and Maine are probably the leaders in woodcock young production, while Wisconsin, Minnesota, Pennsylvania, and the rest of New England have an appreciable amount of habitat for nesting birds, too.

The wintering grounds begin, in the east, on the southern tip of the Delmarva Peninsula, then swing southwest in an arc to northern Alabama, and northwest in an arc to southcentral Missouri. But there's no question that the wintering hotbed for this long-billed challenge is along the banks of the Mississippi,

Woodcock females normally lay four eggs.

before it branches off into the delta near the Gulf of Mexico. Although the bird becomes more popular every year with Louisiana upland enthusiasts, these hunters also have their bobwhite quail, so there's not a great deal of pressure on woodcock around their wintering grounds. This is the antithesis of what happens to other migrators to Louisiana—like pintails, snow geese, mallards, and other waterfowl species.

In the early fall, before serious migration begins, woodcock flit from cover to cover. They may fly north, east, west, or south. Perhaps they are getting in shape like a hunter jogging, or trying to find other members of the clan who'd like to make the long flight south with them. Don't assume that when native birds have vacated your favorite cover the shooting is over. They probably haven't set their wings for Dixie yet. Maybe they've flown upstream or down, across the ridge to the next valley, or to an adjoining county. They may be back in your favored haunt tomorrow, or there may be some new birds that drop in for a rest and a few worms. These newcomers may be from the north, or they might be from the south, east, or west. Later in the fall the woodcocks waste no energy flying any direction but south.

Some new facts are emerging on how to produce woodcock habitat on a large scale, which state game departments are capable of tackling, and on a small scale, where local land-owners can create woodcock habitat at almost no cost, even if they own as little as a few acres. One idea involves cutting strips, maybe twenty or thirty yards wide, through woodcock cover that has become too tall. If this cutting is done on reason-ably moist ground, singing fields are created. In some instances the cutting might involve a minor commercial harvest, but most of it will be a firewood cutting. The landowner can cut his alder and aspen in strips, enjoy the crackling fire in the evening, knowing that come next spring his work will look attractive to returning woodcock.

To keep an area attractive to woodcock, the landowner must keep cutting firewood in strips. The maturing timber will provide the nesting cover, the tracts that were cut four to fifteen years previous will provide the tight cover needed by broods and maturing woodcock, while the newly-cut tracts will provide the singing fields.

The Canadians claim that between 1972 and 1976 there was more than a 25 percent increase in the number of wood-cock hunters. At the same time there was more than a 50 per-cent increase in the number of days spent hunting woodcock in Canada. The woodcock is the number two game animal in New Brunswick, number three in Nova Scotia.

In the United States there's reason to believe that interest in woodcock hunting has also grown by leaps and bounds. Bi-ologists are consequently beginning to wonder about the future of the woodcock. Will this increased pressure affect the overall numbers? Woodcock habitat is dwindling. Flood plains, river bottoms, and stream edges are favored industrial sites, perfect spots for shopping centers or various types of recreation facilities, to say nothing of prime farm lands. These perfect woodcock habitats are being drained and irreparably changed at an alarming rate.

Conversely, the woodcock bag keeps going up, though scientists tell us that woodcock flushes per hour hunted are going down, if very slightly. There's no question that we're losing habitat faster than we're losing our huntable supply of birds. Sooner or later we may have our comeuppance. Will the depletion of habitat catch up with the increase in hunting pressure? To help the biologists, make certain to check every woodcock's leg for a band before placing the bird in your game pouch. They need information to help them keep tabs on population levels and trends. For every one hundred woodcock banded, scientists only get four or five bands returned. This may not be because hunters don't see them or return them, only that 95 percent of the woodcock die a natural death, so no one ever sees those bands.

Americans started shotgunning woodcock shortly after they arrived on these shores with their muzzleloaders. By the late 1700s the use of dogs began to appear in literature. Woodcock were definitely on the sporting scene prior to the Civil War. Prior to the cessation of market hunting with the Migratory Bird Treaty of 1918, woodcock were bringing as much as $1.50. It's unclear whether the hunter pocketed this $1.50 or some middle man. Either way, the price was appreciable. New York restaurant gourmets could expect to plunk down plenty to eat this bird—and this was in the days when a person couldn't walk out of the general store with $1.50 worth of groceries unless he had the help of a boy or two. Obviously, woodcock were considered a delicacy by the gourmets of the day.

They still are, though some people take one bite and push the plate away. Woodcock are different than any other food fare that has ever passed my lips. The meat is rich and filling. I've never seen anyone eat more than a few, though I've heard of those who do. Try filleting the breast off the carcass, one fillet from each side. Place these in warm butter, saute briefly in salt, pepper, and seasoning. Remove from the pan when rare, or, at most, medium rare, while they're still oozing red juices. They are scrumptious, tasting much like beef—and so, so tender.

For those who bag plenty of woodcock and have a number in the freezer, here's a unique way to prepare them. Place them in boiling water for two hours. The meat will then fall from the carcass. Put this tender meat through a food grinder, then mix in either mustard or mayonnaise until the proper consistency is reached, plus salt, pepper, and favored spices. This makes a wonderful sandwich spread or can be used as a pate hors d'oeuvre with crackers. Should you want to add pickles to the spread, put them through the grinder, too.

3

Hunting Grouse Effectively

One particularly thick cutover near home has been extremely productive in recent years. It receives surprisingly little hunting pressure—and I know the reason why. It's a steep sidehill that most hunters are unwilling to tackle. Because it can't be seen from any hard road it is a grouse haven where I've never seen a competitor. Since it is only a twenty-minute drive from my home, I've been hunting this patch about once a week for the last several seasons.

One hunt stands out as the perfect example of the theme for this chapter. Because of both the frustrations involved and the ultimate success of the day, it summarizes what effective grouse hunting is all about. I started off the morning with Star. She was 10½ years old—past her prime physically—but her experience with grouse helped make up for her old age. The hunt had hardly started when Star skidded to a point along-

Star on point in the grouse woods.

side the old tram I was walking. It was midway through the season, and here was a tangle where I had flushed birds previously that year. I was mentally ready.

The bird came up a second or two after Star made the find, trying to fly across the base of a hollow. I was carrying my Franchi 20 autoloader, and it looked like a Low House 5 shot. The first shot, a reload with one ounce of standard 7½s, stopped the bird in mid air, but it was a long shot and the grouse didn't come down. Instead, the bird caught itself. Wings beating furiously and moving at less than top speed, it turned up the little hollow. Startled, I didn't have the presence to send my second load his way, which was a factory-loaded dose of one ounce of copper plated extra hard shot—the Federal Premium.

The bird disappeared from view a half second later, but I held my ground and listened. I heard it hit the ground with a splat. As good as Star is at finding and pointing grouse, she's never been much of a retriever. Anyway, I hurried forward, urging the dog with "Dead bird! Dead bird!" The fall area was strewn with a conglomeration of twisted, rotting limbs, the slash left from the timber operation. The sides of the gully were eroded and steep. Star couldn't get a whiff of scent, though I'm certain I had her scurrying around the fall area.

It was difficult to keep her in close for retrieving. She wanted to range out and find another bird, especially with her adrenalin pumping from the recent flush, but I insisted she stay in. Although the gully sides were steep, they were only about thirty-five feet high. She started working up the left side, appeared to be making game, and I was sure that she would sniff out the wounded grouse momentarily.

Instead, a seemingly unhurt grouse thundered out of the crest, and flew right back across the gully. It was a clear shot, I didn't think there was a twig in his path: a High House 7, the range slightly longer. As I swung, my shotgun intersected the only obstacle in that opening—a big beech snag—and my first shot went directly into it. The second shot went off as the bird disappeared, but it felt good. I knew there was a chance I dropped that bird. But was it the same grouse?

I followed up that second flush immediately, and a seemingly healthy grouse departed as Star and I made the approach to the area where I thought it would be. So it was back to the confines of the little hollow and more searching for the grouse I'd shot first. Already I could feel the back of my shirt was wet with sweat. But there was no scent of a dead or running bird in that hollow. Was it the same bird that flushed again? It sounded to me, when I heard that grouse hit with a splat, that it would never get airborne again. I'll never know.

I had a fair line to where the grouse had flown from flush number three, so I decided to follow up that one. It was a steep uphill climb and I was already soaked with perspiration. Near the top of the hill a bird that had held tight thundered off to my left, almost from underfoot. There weren't any briars here, but the new saplings were young, thin, and twisted together. Before the grouse disappeared from view, I slammed a shot in its direction, and feathers flew.

It was too thick to see the bird come tumbling down. I called Star in. We worked for fifteen more minutes on that bird —feathers in the trees, feathers on the ground, but the dog couldn't get a whiff of scent. It was as if the bird had simply not come down, though the feather evidence was overwhelming.

Now I was really hot. After a thorough search, the dog and I made a circle around the round top. On route, we flushed a bird or two, but there was no shooting. My physical metabolism was still in high, but by talking with myself I was beginning to get control of my frustrations and temper. When we worked back into the area with the feathers on the ground, a bird ripped out from under a tangle and made an escape. Was it the same bird I had perhaps been working on all morning?

I missed with the first shot, and the grouse was behind cover when the second primer was dented. But it tumbled down, rolling back down the hill toward me. Then the grouse turned upright, head bobbing, trying to decide what to do next. I fumbled for another shell. Star was soon in the area— for she knows what shooting means, or can mean!

When I closed the bolt on the autoloader, the grouse flushed again. But this time it had great difficulty getting airborne, and Star was right behind. When it was safe, I slammed my one loaded shell in the general direction—an easy Low House 7 shot—but missed. However, the injured bird came down; Star still in hot pursuit.

Every time the dog got close, the bird would dive under a tangle or juke to the side. Star just couldn't get her jaws on anything but an occasional stray feather. The chase was all downhill, me tripping and half falling in a run that was trying to keep pace. Suddenly the trail ended. I saw where the bird had been. Star simply gave up the chase. Now her age started to show. She was so played out she would do nothing but stand there panting while I encouraged her to find the confounded

dead bird. After she rested a little she caught some of my enthusiasm and made a half-hearted try.

But there was nothing to be found—except more frustration. I had either killed three grouse that morning and hadn't
found a one, or this one Super Grouse had nine lives. It seemed
there was no way I could ever get him in my game bag. The
old canine campaigner was played out anyway, so, disgusted,
I heeled her back to the car and exchanged her for Grouse
Magic, a three-year-old pointer who is an outstanding retriever.
I kept Magic at heel as I trudged halfway up the long hill, then
turned her loose where Star had lost the track. Magic made
one circle, and, when she came back, she snuffed out Super
Grouse from under the leaves—practically under my feet!

What an exhilarating feeling it was to pocket that one.
Had Star caught up with the bird during our high speed chase
and provided the coup de grace with one chomp? It seemed
impossible, since she was always within sight. But if that's
what happened, it explains why she lost interest and started
panting instead of looking. She's one of those bird dogs who
only finds the bird, doesn't pick it up and bring it back. This is
a major grouse dog fault, but I love that Star just the same.
Her outstanding redeeming quality is her heart; she hunts like
a demon.

Magic and I went back to scouring other areas on that steep
hillside cover. The birds were there, but I was always in the
wrong place at the wrong time. The result was no second bird
to fill the state limit. Killing two grouse can be easy, but not
every day. Some states have more generous grouse limits—five
a day. I revel in hunting one or more of these states every year.
In many of them, the walking is over pleasant terrain, not the
muscle wearying mountain covers close to my home.

With one dog or another I tramped and clawed my way
through briars, tangles, blowdowns, and thorns for six hours.
I paid a price in limb-whipped ears, briar-scratched cheeks
and wrists, thorn-probed thighs, and vines bent on tripping
tired legs, but I couldn't connect.

As I was making one last uphill trudge near the end of the

day, the payoff came. Luck or fate took me right to the bird, which roared out at close range. The cover was super thick, but I still had the diminutive 20 at the port arms, and the first charge sent this one spinning. I sat down exhausted at the spot where he landed, picked him up, smoothed his feathers and raised my eyebrows toward the sky. Soon Star was beside me, sniffing the dead bird and looking for her reward. Suddenly the day's tramp was more worthwhile than ever. But it was over. Star knew it, too. I didn't even have to tell her to heel. We eased back toward the pickup at a slow pace—satisfied, fulfilled, and tired—oh so tired.

No matter where this bird is hunted, the grouse is wing-shooting's toughest target. The bird is cunningly calculating, a challenge that goes beyond any other game bird on the face of the earth. The only reason every hunter in the world doesn't pursue them is that the grouse is simply too much trouble, too much effort for most hunters. But a grouse nut knows what is called for and he's willing to put out—for a crumb of reward here and there.

Before the woodcock have headed south, I seldom have trouble bagging a limit of five. Quail hunters in good country sometimes bag hundreds of birds each season. Ringneck routers usually bag a brace within a few hours if they're hunting habitat with birds. But grouse hunters might tramp the most damnable terrain all day long and not get a decent shot. The grouse offers a different challenge than most other upland critters; and those who dive into tangles with vigor may not number in legions, but they make up in enthusiasm what they lack in numbers.

Preparing for Hunting Season

It's a good idea to spend the weeks of late summer getting into better physical condition for the upcoming grousing marathons. Jogging is an excellent way to accomplish this, but I hate it. I stay in fair shape for level walking year round. I sel-

Lawrence Cignetti and his son Joe with a Pennsylvania limit of birds.

dom get tired hunting flat woodcock bottoms until I've put in five or more hours. Since I always open Pennsylvania's upland season with woodcock forays, these walks over relatively level alder, crab, and aspen-covered bottoms get my legs in shape for the later, tougher going on grouse after the tims have departed. Because I'm able to hunt every day, seven to ten woodcock outings have my leg muscles well prepared for the hillier grouse walks. This may not be a practical approach for the average hunter, however. Jogging is certainly an answer for those who can put up with the boredom.

Once in the grouse woods, the pace of the hunt becomes extremely important. I learned pace from my hunting partner of many years, Lawrence Cignetti. He was more than thirty-five years my senior, but even in his late sixties he showed me what being able to walk in the woods was all about. Every time I looked in his direction, he was ahead and I had to extend extra effort to catch up. But Cignetti never hurried. His walk was like the staccato patter of water dripping from a roof. It was steady, the same one hour as the next, the same at the start of the day as at the end.

Being in good physical condition is a necessity, but a mental toughness is even more important. It's this unrelenting mental attitude, coupled with a never-get-discouraged enthusiasm, that permits some hunters to go on walking hour after hour while others have given up and headed for the nearest pub. The true grouse hunter acquires the right attitude, maintains a constant pace, and rounds it out with good physical well-being.

The neophyte grouser goes to the woods hoping to find game. The knowledgeable grouse hunter enters the woods knowing he's going to flush his share of ruffs. Unless it's been for a half-hour hunt, I've never gone grouse hunting and not found anything. But I've spent a lifetime learning where grouse live. In my part of the country, grouse live in abandoned farms and cut-over slashings. They feed on red dogwood berries, grey dogwood fruit, crabs, grapes, greens, and aspen buds. I

Grey dogwood.

know what time of the year they switch from one food to another, and all expert grousers know these things.

It's this overall knowledge that permits a hunter to know when he's found a promising patch of cover—before he ever enters it. Although there are habitat generalities that describe the grouse's range, there are also local peculiarities that help the individual hunter find more birds.

Grey dogwood is a good example. In recent years these berries have been tremendously abundant during the first half of Pennsylvania's season. Consequently, I make mental notes about where I find concentrations of these berries, then I hunt them thoroughly. The same goes for red dogwood berries, the fruit of the flowering dogwood. In years when red berries are hanging in big clumps, I search out sidehills where I've observed the white flowers the previous May.

Wild raspberries are another favorite grouse food when they are available. Though grouse seldom find this food in my bailiwick, I flush plenty of birds from this type of cover in more northern latitudes. The same goes for apples. When woodcock hunting with guide Arlie Day near McAdam, New Brunswick, I would hear Arlie blurt out occasionally, "Apple tree ahead!" It was uncanny, but virtually every time he did, we soon had a grouse going out.

Do you know what an aspen tree looks like, a hawthorn, or any other of the trees and bushes that grouse are known to feed on or live around? If you don't, make it your business to learn. The result will be not only more interesting tramps afield, you'll flush and pocket more grouse.

Once the grey dogwood berries have fallen to the ground, the birds have them devoured within a few days. There's no sense hunting this type of cover any longer, you'll be wasting your time. Know where to look next. What will the grouse be feeding on when one prime food source is gone?

The quickest avenue to learning what grouse feed on is to closely examine crop contents. When Cignetti returned from a grouse hunt, he fed his dogs, had a filling supper, then went to

The contents of the grouse's crop will reveal what the bird has been eating. Here are crops from two grouse, spread near a male's fantail.

his garage to clean the birds. Many hunters detest, or at least dislike, getting the critters they kill ready for the freezer. Cignetti loved it.

The first thing he'd do would be to spread newspaper, open the bird's crop, and spill the contents onto the paper. (Gallinaceous birds like grouse hold recently ingested food in a receptacle located in the neck area. It is swallowed into the stomach at some later time.) Then he'd pick the various foods apart, identifying each berry and green. He'd remember where he flushed the bird, recalling if the food in the crop was nearby. If he couldn't identify something in the bird's crop, he studied, asked, and worked at it until he had the answer. Lawrence knew a lot about where to go at any given time after a lifetime study of what birds ate. Any hunter who doesn't investigate the crop of every bird he kills is missing out on some of the most important information available about effective grouse hunting.

How To Hunt The Area

Planning the hunt strategy before the hunt starts is an excellent idea. Unless I'm hunting with a young dog I'm training, I like to walk overgrown tram roads when I work a young slashing. My experienced dogs know how to quarter from one side to the other. I'm still busting some brush, but I'm in a more advantageous shooting position on the tram.

Most days I plan how I'll walk into the area via one tram, circle via another, out via another, hit another area via a gully, etc.—all this before I leave the vehicle or as I'm walking into the hunting grounds. Many times my course will be altered, usually to follow up a bird; but by starting with a game plan, I begin my hunt in the most effective manner.

I follow up on 95 percent of the grouse I flush and doing so is another important point of this chapter. Many factors contribute to increased success in finding grouse that are followed up. Remember to watch every grouse that flushes—whether or not you shoot—as intently as possible, for as long as possible. Then keep looking for several more seconds in case the bird can be glimpsed one more time. The tyro remembers all this after the grouse has gone.

The more information your eyes can give you with regard to where the grouse is flying, the better your chances of flushing him again and being in position for a better shot than the one just missed. Your ears are important, too. Many grouse flushes are heard and not seen, especially in the early part of the season when foliage is extra-thick. By stopping and listening intently as soon as the roar of wings is heard, the hunter can still get a good line on the bird's direction.

It's particularly helpful if the hunter knows the cover well. On some flushes I have such a good idea of where the grouse is flying that I'd be willing to bet a box of coppered 8s on it. This comes not only from knowledge of the cover, but from remembering where birds flew when flushed from a particular spot on previous occasions. No one reflushes every bird, but the ability to find a high percentage of them translates into an important success statistic—more grouse flushed per hour.

Many grouse shots are taken just as the bird disappears from view. When that happens always pause for several seconds, listening intently. On most occasions you'll be able to hear the bird hit the ground if you've made a telling shot. Or you'll often hear his departing wings keep on beating if you missed. The natural thing to do after a shot as the bird disappears is to swear or take several steps ahead or to the side in an effort to see something. Quell both urges, or learn to. Train yourself to remain stationary after such a shot and listen —you'll pocket several more birds every season.

Steep territory does not lend itself to following up all birds. If a grouse is flushed on a crest you can bet he's going to head downhill. If he's flushed at the base of a valley there's a better than even chance he'll head for the peak. Southcentral Ohio offers some great grouse hunting, but it's only for the stoic. Hunters who haven't been there may envision Ohio as flat farm country, but the southcentral part of the state is anything but flat.

Instead of constantly following grouse uphill or down in this tough cover, many steep-hill-country hunters, especially in years when grouse populations are fairly high, walk the sidehills at one elevation. Maybe three hunters will spread out on a hill, each staying at the same level as they progress. They work along the side, making the indentation at each hollow along the hill, each maintaining the same elevation as they walk. This is a worthwhile and much less fatiguing way to hunt. In any reasonable terrain, however, it pays to follow up those grouse, for as long as you can keep finding them.

Many hunters keep returning, year after year, to areas long past their prime. It's natural to dream about recapturing the thrills once enjoyed on a hunt when the birds were roaring out of every tangle. But that urge must be tempered with common sense. Grouse are birds of a regenerating forest, not of a maturing one. While they might be found occasionally in an old favored spot that is growing high, this will be the exception to the rule.

By the same token, once you find a heavily populated area, don't hold off hunting it in hopes you'll save the grouse for future years. Don't hunt such a spot every day because the birds will become too wary, but pound it regularly—maybe once a week. Grouse cannot be stockpiled. There are going to be a certain number of birds there next year—whether you hunt them a lot or a little this year.

If you do visit an old haunt and notice that the habitat is changing and becoming too high for grouse, it's a good idea to strike out from the familiar area to the surrounding grounds that you don't know well. I have discovered numerous new coverts by relying on this formula. In point of fact, I found the thick sidehill referred to at the start of this story in that manner.

To further increase your effectiveness in the grouse woods, check the outdoor magazines for grouse hunting pieces. They may appear year round, but editors particularly like to use grouse stories in the fall months. Keep an eye out for information on states or locales where grouse are especially plentiful. Maybe you can plan a trip there. Also be on the lookout for useful how-to information. Maybe an expert has come up with a new technique that produces for him.

No matter what you do, the grouse is a tough customer. It takes a lot to put this bird in the game pouch. But this is one of the major factors that makes grouse buffs so devoted to their bird. No matter who you are or where you hunt, when you pick up a dead grouse and smooth his feathers, wishing you could put him back like a fly-caught trout, it's a moment to remember and treasure, a moment for reflection and thanksgiving. But you know you earned that bird and that moment because you worked so long and so hard for them.

4

Hunting Woodcock
Effectively

It's important for upland enthusiasts to realize that grouse and woodcock require different tactics. Admittedly, woodcock can be sacked on grouse tramps, and vice versa. But to be most successful on woodcock hunts, some changes from grouse techniques need to be incorporated. The last chapter covered effective grouse hunting techniques. Most good grouse hunters strike out across bird country with purpose. With a steady pace they cover acre after acre, turning only to follow a flush, otherwise going in one direction all the time.

Woodcock hunting requires a different style. I feel it's important to twist and turn, going back over patches that seem to be tramped out. On opening day I hunt one special flood plain, and I have done so for over fifteen years. As woodcock covers go, it's a big one—maybe two hundred acres—although the prime 'doodle spots cover a much more restricted acreage.

Although I walk fast, I usually spend five hours in this thicket. Yet I can walk from one end to the other, flushing one to three birds in less than half an hour. By constantly turning rather than maintaining a straight course, by crisscrossing back and forth, I not only cover this long-bill haven completely, I constantly find birds—some that the dogs and I have passed by

Hunter swings on fast-flushing woodcock.

previously, some that have flushed and landed in an area after we've passed through, some that simply move back quickly to their favored haunts.

I hunt almost every timberdoodle patch in a similar manner. If you want to increase your effectiveness on this bird, try my attack. Woodcock coverts are often small. A one-hundred-acre cover is big. Many are less than a half acre, yet hold one to four birds. A quail covey dog hunts a half acre in about three seconds. He won't find many long bills. It takes thoroughness and patience to seek out this secretive, tight sitter.

The fact that many woodcock sit especially tight is another reason for crisscrossing and rehunting a previously covered area. It's easy to walk very close to one of these birds and not have them budge. Many dogs are anxious and rangy. A closer, more thorough worker has better luck with tims. But in the morning most dogs are so full of vim and vigor that it's tough or impossible to keep them in as close as you want—yet another reason for rehunting, recrisscrossing, and rechecking. Level walking is often a part of timberdoodle chasing, a welcome change of pace (literally) compared to some of the steep grouse haunts I tramp every season. Northwestern Pennsylvania is almost as flat as the average skeet field, and I never became fatigued sauntering across one of them.

Hunting Techniques

Woodcock hunting companions should be chosen carefully, especially if you subscribe to the twist and turn method that is so effective in small covers. Both the hunter and the companion must maintain the same pace. With turns made constantly, each must know exactly where the other is. If this practice isn't adhered to judiciously, both will be forced to pass up most of the shots presented by flushing tims, or, perish the thought, one of the duo might shoot the other.

I hunt woodcock alone most of the season, but one partner I always welcome is Scott Harrison. We live about four hours apart, but we've known each other since grade school, so there's always a great deal to relive when we get together. The past doesn't make him a suitable woodcock companion, but his knowledge of cover and his hunting habits, which are similar to mine, make us ideal partners. When we're tramping an alder or aspen patch we combine forces to send the long-billed quarry airborne. There are fewer birds in every haven when we depart.

Telltale feather on ground after shot indicates a dead woodcock nearby.

Scott's home hunting country is a pheasant valhalla—much more open terrain than the woodcock haunts we tramp on opening day. If anything, I have to slow Scott down a little at the start, but he adjusts remarkably well. We try to stay close together, not amble off thirty or forty yards from each other. It's so thick on opening day we sometimes can't see one another when we're ten yards away, let alone thirty. But if we're close, we can hear one another. I'm constantly looking in his direction to make sure where he is. Even more important from my viewpoint, I want to make sure he knows where I am. I don't want to send any pellets in his direction, and I don't want him sending any my way either! This latter point is one that is often forgotten by some hunters. If I don't see Scott, or any other compatriot I might be with in 'doodle country, I call out; then we work closer together. Calling out not only helps me find where he is, it helps me be sure my shooting friend knows where I am.

Rich Drury, champion skeet shooter, and I also get along well in woodcock cover. He's safety conscious and willing to adapt to my twist and turn hunting style. (He also has a good dog. That's an important reason for inviting someone on a hunt, too.) The first time we ever hunted together I talked him into a long drive to northwestern Pennsylvania and some top aspen and crab apple covers I know in that area.

Rich and I first tried a patch that has produced a number of memorable hunts for me, even though getting to the prime part of the cover is always a hassle. The best spot is a thirty-acre tract of young aspen; but to reach it, a very boggy swamp must be traversed. The fact that two or three steps in this bog are guaranteed to go over the boot tops is only a small part of the problem. That swamp is so thick it sometimes takes an hour of cursing, sweating, and bleeding to get through—but it's worth it. That aspen tangle is loaded with birds more often than not. If the sun is out, I can sometimes cross the swamp in less than an hour. If it's cloudy, it takes longer (because my compass is always back in my pickup). There are no hills or ridges in this flat country, so it's difficult to keep the direction straight in the thicket.

When we finally made it into that patch last season, Drury's new shirt looked like I. M. Hipp's tear-away after several stalwart linebackers had manhandled it. The birds weren't there like they should have been, but we found several, making the tramp worthwhile. If memory serves me right, Rich bagged three and I pocketed two in about two hours. I have killed a limit of five in twenty minutes on several previous occasions there, however. We took two hours to hunt that patch because we crisscrossed back and forth time after time.

By the time we'd given it a good going over almost three hours had elapsed. (It took a long while to fight through the swamp.) Then we had to battle our way back through the almost impenetrable swale to reach my pickup. Once I thought I was going to have to apply a tourniquet to Rich's bleeding wrist, but then a fierce limb whipped his cheek and made him forget about the blood dripping from his arm and soaking his new, well-torn shirt.

At the truck we lounged in the grass, munched a sandwich, and savored an apple while our wounds healed.

"Rich, I know another spot up the road a couple of miles, and we won't have to cross one of these damnable swamps to reach it. We still have time. Let's give it a try." I was beginning to think my briar-pricked thighs might survive after all.

Drury squinted at me cautiously and suspiciously, checked the caked blood on his one wrist, rubbed his still sore cheek, then gave me one-half of the victory sign.

"Honest. It won't be as bad this time. Cover's thick, but nothing like that swamp that almost swallowed us."

Reluctantly he got into my pickup, mumbling something about hitchhiking home with his shorthair. But he's a shooter, and I knew he wouldn't be able to stand the thought of me banging away at fast-flushing birds while he stood on the interstate with his thumb out. (See the introduction to chapter 10, *Woodcock Weaponry* for the serialized conclusion to that day afield. It too involved constant twisting and turning.)

When I worked in a steel mill, one of my fellow foremen asked me to take him bird hunting. I knew it would be a fiasco, but he insisted. It was hot, typical for early season woodcock hunting. When I picked him up I told him he had too many clothes on, but he said he hated to get cold.

We hunted the flood plain backwaters of a local reservoir. The water level had been reduced quickly the previous winter when heavy ice covered those flood plains. The result was crushed vegetation everywhere we tramped. This phenomenon (not unusual around many reservoirs) made the walking difficult. It seemed as though all the vegetation was crushed and bent over between our knees and our eyes. At leg level it meant forcing our way through; at chest level it meant bending over to get through.

These conditions made ideal cover for the birds. I was doing very well because I knew what to expect. I was carrying a five-pound 20-gauge at the port arms, so I was ready for the fast shots. I was wearing a light cotton shirt and thin vest, though my pants were reasonably briar-proof. Phil carried an eight-pound autoloader, wore a wool shirt and canvas coat. Perspiration beaded at his forehead, soaked his shirt, and sent his metabolism skyrocketing. One hour was all he could stand.

"Where's the car? Get me out of here. I've seen every bit of your damn woodcock hunting that I ever want to see."

I made sure we departed in a roundabout way—roundabout enough that I shot my limit of five tims before my pickup came into view. But that was Phil's last 'doodle chase.

Woodcock hunting means traveling in very thick cover, often in high temperatures. Timberdoodles head south when cold weather approaches. By the time the leaves are down, they're gone. That's when I turn to grouse, which are almost impossible to bag when the foliage is still hanging heavy. I don't feel I lose a thing by not hunting them earlier. In ten to

Expect good woodcock cover to be extremely thick.

fourteen days I've had all the woodcock hunting I need, so I'm
ready for a change.

As in grouse chasing, following up flushes is of paramount
importance. The primary key to reflushing birds is watching
and listening. When a bird goes out, don't take your eyes off it
merely because you miss or can't get a shot. Watch closely,

then keep watching to catch another glimpse. Many woodcock fly only twenty or thirty yards, then they sit right down. Most fly farther, but these birds usually skirt the low tree tops for only a short distance before parachuting.

Although long bills might helicopter up from an extremely thick tangle the first time you send them airborne, they consistently land in an opening. Sometimes they sit down in a circle only a foot or two in diameter, but they can't get back down to earth in the thicker parts of the territory they inhabit. When following up a bird, be certain to check out every little opening in the cover you come to, and be ready at such a spot— both physically (with the gun) and mentally (so you can react quickly).

By watching closely I've seen an untold number of woodcock descending into cover. If I hadn't been watching attentively, and for as long, I would have had only a good line on the bird. By watching more closely I often know exactly where to go.

Sometimes these birds can't be seen when they flush. Stop your forward movement and listen. You can't hear if you keep plowing brush. The twitter of woodcock wings often permits the attentive hunter to learn which direction the quarry has flown.

The ability to reflush a high percentage of woodcock will directly reflect on the yearly bag. Those who reflush plenty will kill plenty. Those who only reflush the occasional bird will enjoy minimal success.

Woodcock Cover

A thorough knowledge of the cover aids greatly in improving reflush statistics. Several years ago I hunted a nearby county with the local game protector. Since he had been good enough to show me some fine covers in his bailiwick, I invited him to shoot some of mine with me the following October. He brought his young son along. That was Mark's first hunting season and

Hunter swings on woodcock that has been flushed from the thicket by a companion hunter. This hunter, walking along the edge, is in the right position for an open shot as the bird tries to fly from one thick spot to another.

his very first bird hunt. His Dad had put him through many clay target fun sessions, and the boy had graduated from a hunter safety course.

After we fought brush for a couple of hours, Mark still hadn't broken the ice with his first woodcock, though his Dad had a brace and I had three. While following up one of the reflushes I instructed young Mark, "That woodcock we just flushed should be in that little opening ahead. It's too thick for them to land where we are right now. That break in the cover has been the first spot open enough to provide a landing field." The dog was off to the left, sniffing out something interesting, and though I'd called her in close, she hadn't responded.

We were tramping a patch that I knew as well as my basement, having hunted it once or twice a year for fifteen years, and having enjoyed a number of dog training sessions there. Mark walked into the edge of the opening with his light 20-gauge at the ready, but was still a little surprised when the tim took off right where I had predicted it would. That woodcock was Mark's first score on feathered targets, so he was elated. He still thinks I'm sort of a wizard because I had that bird pinned as well with my knowledge, know how, and experience as any sharp pointing dog would have with his nose.

Don't forget to check for dead woodcock in trees. The first time this happened to me I was behind Radar, a shorthair. I toppled the 'doodle in plain view. Radar was a great retriever, but he couldn't get a whiff of that woodcock. But I was persistent. I kept looking long beyond the reasonable time period, even went back to where I'd taken the shot to make doubly certain I was looking in the right place. I was. I wasn't smart enough to look up for about twenty minutes, and that was by accident. The bird was wedged in the fork of a small sapling. No wonder the dog couldn't smell it. That incident occurred about sixteen years ago. Since then I've pocketed quite a number of woodcock that hung in vegetation and never made it to the ground. Don't give up looking for a woodcock you're sure is down without checking the surrounding trees.

I feel there are two types of woodcock covers—one for flight birds and another for natives. Although both types of birds certainly use the same covers from time to time, there are usually subtle differences. As a rule, flight woodcock are reluctant to move far off their migratory route, so they drop into covers along their way that might not be ideal. On the other hand, local birds have all summer and early fall to seek out perfect hides and feeding grounds that are usually off the beaten path. Also, native woodcock tend to hold in smaller patches, along minor stream beds, flood plains, etc., while migratory birds tend to touch down on the ridges, in valleys of major rivers, on high plateaus. Before I leave home in the morning I know whether I'm going to be hunting native birds or their migrating cousins.

The woodcock patches near my home are not near any major migration routes, but I do a lot of hunting in northwestern Pennsylvania, which is a top area of natives. The migratory flights sometimes involve tremendous numbers of birds. Still, there are subtle differences in the covers these birds use. Learning those differences can help you become a more effective hunter.

In most states local birds are hunted at the start of the season, the first flights usually starting a week or two later. There's little sense in hunting a cover noted for its appeal to migratory birds before they start heading south. When they aren't migrating, it pays to concentrate on local birds.

I hunt covers where I expect to find native birds without regard to the weather report. When I have time to hunt I simply head for a good covert. But hunting flight birds is another matter entirely. I have one or two friends who hunt woodcock, and they live along a major migration route, so I stay in touch with them when I know the time is near. I also watch national weather closely, for woodcock often fly south on the leading edge of a front—usually one out of the north or northwest that's laden with frigid air off the Arctic ice cap.

Any hunter who has been lucky enough to be afield when

a genuine flight touches down is indeed lucky. This is an experience every uplander should enjoy. But this is feast or famine hunting, no matter how closely you watch that weather map. While you might take a limit in less than half an hour when the birds are in, you probably won't get a shot the following day. Though the ground may be covered with their white, chalky calling card, it was Dixie those long bills had in mind.

The major reason I concentrate a lot of my tim hunting around flood plains of flood control reservoirs centers around the ice effect. A few pages back I mentioned how the ice had knocked down a lot of cover in a patch where I took a tyro and quickly tired him out. All reservoirs north of the Mason-Dixon Line freeze over every year, especially the shallow backwaters that are flooded during high water. As soon as the threat of one flood is over, the engineers at the flood control dams start preparing for the next rain storm. They do this by releasing water from above the dam as quickly and as safely as they can. This happens repeatedly through the spring. On many flood plains a film of ice one to two inches thick will cover the vegetation. Although this doesn't happen every year, it occurs often. The result is ice that kills and crushes down the vegetation on the flood plain as the water level is lowered, effectively permitting new cover to grow every time it happens. This means that these covers have a much longer life with respect to woodcock appeal. Any flood control dams in your area should be checked out for both the abundance of woodcock cover and the effect ice has on the habitat.

But no matter how much the ice outs prolong ideal habitat conditions for woodcock, the patch is certain to become less and less productive over the years. Patches not affected by ice will have an even shorter life. In many instances, woodcock habitat will last longer than grouse habitat, but there's a need to constantly search out new places to hunt tims. This realization is always the mark of the outstanding hunter.

One good time to check out and look for new cover is in the spring when the birds are returning. Woodcock use the same flight routes whether they're flying north or south, and the local birds return to the same patches they probed the previous fall. Dogs have a fine time in March, sniffing for returning tims, honing their olfactory skills. Hunters shouldn't always return to their October haunts at that time of year, though. Finding new plots will mean more fun and more birds the following fall. Because the leaves are down in the spring the hunter has a more open landscape to investigate. This means that learning more about habitat and habits becomes easier.

I once thought that a grouse cover could never be overhunted, but I'm beginning to question that premise. It has been my experience that hard hunting of ruffed grouse habitats makes the birds so smart and edgy that hunting them becomes futile. Although shooting a cover out may be all but impossible, grouse become so wary if pursued relentlessly that scoring becomes virtually impossible. They might as well not be there at all as far as the hunter is concerned.

Woodcock cover can be overshot. Have no compunctions about harvesting a limit of migratory birds from a small patch. You won't be harming the future a bit, but beware of overshooting a local haunt of natives. Like salmon returning to the stream and pool where they were born, woodcock do essentially the same. Remember that several more birds may be harvested from that cover by other hunters, plus they'll be pursued by still others as they make their way south, and yet again by still more gunners once they reach the South. This doesn't take natural mortality into account either. Accordingly, I don't hunt a woodcock cover more than once or twice per season. Others should protect their coverts in a similar manner.

A ready gun carry and a ready mental attitude will also help the woodcock devotee be more effective. Once the shot is taken a pause is suggested. Listen for the gentle fall in case the bird disappeared from view as the trigger was squeezed.

While many consider themselves combination hunters who pursue both grouse and woodcock, it's important to remember that these two birds abide in differing habitats and require different techniques if one expects to be successful with any degree of consistency. To be sure, their habitat does overlap. Once in Ohio I had a rare opportunity for a double, both a woodcock and a grouse in the air at the same time. I missed the grouse but bagged the long bill. That duo flush proved one of the many exceptions, however. While specialized techniques will provide the grouse hunter with more fun and action, a different set of rules govern how the woodcock devotee should pursue this bird. The ability to switch back and forth with these tactics is the mark of the true grouse and woodcock hunter.

5

Finding Grouse

Searching for new grouse territory can be exciting. Maybe there's a little Christopher Columbus in every good grouse hunter who enjoys exploring new country and revels in new discovery. That's the way I felt one December 7.

The season in my home state was closed because deer hunting was still open; but in neighboring Ohio, partridge hunters were welcome. I chose the northeastern part of the Buckeye State because it was only a three-hour drive, the early fall reports from the Ohio Department of Natural Resources claimed plenty of birds, and the terrain is flat so the hunt would not be physically taxing.

I had two pointers along—Star, my old timer, and Magic, a top three-year-old dog. The first promising patch was located after only a few minutes of exploring. There was a big clump of grey dogwood next to the road. It still held a multitude of cream-colored berries at the top of the stalks. This was unusual for that late in the season.

Magic got the first crack. I was shooting my 20-gauge Franchi. The day was moderate in temperature, heavily over-cast, and threatening rain. The previous days had been ex-tremely cold.

I swung the anxious pointer around to the downwind side of the grey dogwood stems, then motioned her in that direction. Ten feet later she was locked solid as a bank vault. I skirted the right side of the spindly vegetation, and the ruff rocketed forward. If I had been one step farther before it flushed, I would have had a perfect shot. But the bird departed just before the ideal time, so all I had was a quick shot. It flew over the country road, topped the high pines on the opposite side, and disappeared. My snap shot failed to connect.

Rather than follow the bird into those tall conifers, I coaxed the dog in the opposite direction. From the road it looked like a slashing lay beyond, and I meant to have a look. As we eased back into the heart of that covert I made up my mind I'd try it the following September for woodcock. It looked like ideal timberdoodle country, and the Ohio Department of Natural Resources opens their tim season a month before Pennsylvania. This is according to guidelines set up by the federal biologists. Ohio falls under the Mississippi Flyway regulations, Pennsyl-vania those of the Atlantic Flyway.

While I was dreaming about warmer weather and the start of another season, Magic brought me back to the current mo-ment, locking into a staunch point next to a blowdown that reeked of grouse. I circled, trying to get the bird between the dog and me. A grouse went out off to my left, but I didn't have a shot. Magic stayed just as mesmerized while I became less alert. She's steady to wing and shot, so I figured she had not heard the ruff flush.

The bird she smelled was right under her nose, however. It bored into towering flight. I would have had a quick open shot if I had reacted quickly enough, but I was mistakenly

Magic sniffs out a grouse.

relaxed because of the first flush. My 7½s were mostly spent trying to drive their way through super-thick limbs. Moral? Always believe your dog.

There were one or more additional moments of action before we got back to the pickup. Nothing to produce an overdose of adrenalin, but at least I had found birds in an area I'd never hunted before. Five minutes of driving and the pickup was adjacent to another logged-over area. It was Star's turn. The cover wasn't big, and we only found one bird. I should have bagged it as it wheeled out of the thick cover where the dog and I were. It whirred across fairly open pasture, then topped the trees beyond—whose trunks were nailed intermittently with "No Trespass" posters. My pellets were directed too far toward the posterior end of that grouse.

I parked at the next promising patch because of the abundance of grapevines. I reasoned that the recent harsh weather might have forced the birds to take refuge in a haven where they had the escape cover, so essential in winter when a lack of vegetation makes them much more vulnerable to hunters and four-legged and winged predators. Also, they would have to move only a few feet to gorge on the plentiful grapes.

Magic got her second chance. We tramped from one end to the other before she smelled her first. It was pinned under a deadfall that was fairly open around the spot. It looked like a sure thing. I had one good shot, but it didn't connect. Disappointed that I'd failed again to reward the dog for a job well done, I followed that one up—and found it near a field edge, but it drilled out ahead before I was close enough. The flight path took it right along the edge, so I figured chances were good for flushing that one again.

It was in a thick entanglement of vines. The dog winded it from afar but hadn't pointed yet. I was ready. To give me every possible chance that cocky grouse hopped up on a limb amidst the viney jungle and dared me to take him sitting. Then in mockery it flushed across the open weed field, my pellets killing nothing but dark red, winter-dormant grapevines. I followed that bird again, but it evidently had enough of fooling with me for one day. I never saw it again.

I had been hunting for almost three hours up until then, including the time spent in all three covers. In that interim I had flushed seven grouse. Hardly a banner day, but then all hell broke loose when I dove into the center of a thirty-acre patch where the grapevines were concentrated. I found the spot by accident.

Magic and I were close to the pickup, and I almost went to it, planning to look for one more cover before starting the long drive back. But it looked like thicker vines loomed in the distance. Magic was headed that way.

She skidded to a halt as the first grouse went out at the speed of a Mach I. I eased in closer, cautioning her to hold, hoping there might be another. There was, but his exit speed approached Mach II. I couldn't get the little 20 to my shoulder.

When grouse number three went out at full speed, my heart started pounding.

Magic moved forward slowly, tail swishing back and forth, nose sweeping right to left, inhaling deeply. Her nostrils caught the scent, her tail stiffened like a poker, her right front paw cocked upward, her entire body was motionless. Five seconds later a hen bird emerged at what I considered more normal speed. I only had a flash shot as the grouse rose above the vegetation. The 7½s went directly to the mark, however, and Magic soon had her prize wedged gently between her jaws—one down.

The next hour and a half provided some of the most action-packed periods I've ever experienced in the grouse woods. During that ninety minutes I counted nineteen flushes. Many of them were reflushes, to be sure. But what made the day especially worthwhile was the fact that these birds in the thick vines were willing to sit tight. For the day I had more than one dozen solid points on grouse. I can't reach back in memory to recall a day when the dogs had better luck. The total flush rate for the day was twenty-six, but it was the nineteen in the last hour and a half that had my blood boiling with excitement.

Ohio's limit that year was three birds, and that's the only reason I stopped hunting. By the time I pocketed my third grouse I was still enjoying a fantastic flush rate. All three grouse came off points, too. The second was a follow-up of a reflush. Magic had worked this one perfectly, nailing it under a small log just outside the thick grapevines. The grouse held extremely tight while I walked in, going out almost at my feet.

His escape path took him quartering to the left, but it was an easy shot. He took the center of the pattern. There were several more points in the interim, but Magic smelled my final bird at the last instant. Why the grouse held so tight when the dog approached so close, I'll never know. Her nose was less than a foot away from the entanglement of vines where the grouse was holding.

Magic performed admirably with a dozen solid points in a short period of time.

I was ready for this one, though it still held for unending seconds. I wondered if the dog wasn't pointing to where a bird had just departed. Finally the cock lost his nerve. I don't know when I've ever killed a bird quicker. He died five feet from his last perch.

What a day! Talk about success! I had sought out new bird country and found it—far beyond my expectations. Reaching back into past experience, I reasoned which type of cover the birds would be hiding in that day and they were there. The dog training had paid off, for Magic had shown what she was capable of. My shooting practice had paid off—even though I missed several birds before I started to connect. I'll remember that day for a long time.

Paradoxically, I went back to those same three covers later in December and only flushed five grouse in three and a half hours. Although I did manage to bag one of them, it was a far less successful hunt. But the weather had turned much colder, several inches of snow covered the ground, and it was Christmas vacation—which meant youngsters and teachers were on woodland tramps as well as the normal number of grouse hunters. I've always found that locating grouse was more difficult in bad weather. When I do find them under inclement conditions they're usually wild, flushing far ahead of both the dogs and me. Added pressure makes them more touchy, too.

My whole point of that exciting Ohio hunt has been to illustrate that grouse love grapes and grapevines—some of the time, anyway. This fact may be no revelation, but the premise is so important that it needs to be continually mentioned and proven. Grouse tangles are not inviting to those thinly clad, but no true grouse hunter will pass up one of these jungles.

Grapes don't abound everywhere. They're particularly plentiful in the Appalachians, while New England and midwest ruff buffs seldom find this food or vegetation in abundance. In the Midwest the prime grouse habitat is aspen, but it must be in the right stage of development.

It looks like there's an almost endless supply of aspen in southern Canada, and in Michigan, Wisconsin and Minnesota.

If this wood becomes an important industrial fuel source during the 1980s and 1990s, look for grouse populations to respond favorably. This could be the greatest boon to hunting since the timber barons of yesteryear devastated practically every stick of wood to be had. But this time it won't be devastation. Tracts of aspen will be cut but encouraged to quickly grow back. The more this happens, the higher grouse populations are destined to climb. Equally important, this management of the forest will also enhance the habitat for white-tailed deer, cottontail and snowshoe rabbits, and other game and non-game species.

Michigan is one state I try to hunt every year. Their Department of Natural Resources does a tremendous job managing aspen for the benefit of game. The state owns numerous tracts of land, and they cut timber on an ambitious basis. I wish other states would manage their lands as effectively.

When they clear-cut a tract, it's usually a small one—maybe thirty acres. They don't cut mature, mast-producing species because they know these foods are important to most wildlife. They often disc the soil to encourage root suckers of aspen to sprout. In one management area in Gladwin County, a special dog training tract where several grouse championships are held, they've had phenomenal success—as much as ten thousand aspen trees to the acre the first year.

The beauty of hunting Michigan and the other two midwest states mentioned is the generally level terrain one usually encounters. Another plus in hunting Michigan is their county maps, which the Department of Natural Resources offers to the public at nominal cost. Most roads are laid out in squares, and every road is shown on these maps, as are the state-owned lands. It's easy to drive the back country roads and check the state land (always open to public hunting) to see if any recent cutting has taken place. Once I locate a couple of promising covers, I study my maps at the motel each evening, planning where I'll hunt the next day and how I'll get there by taking a roundabout route that will take me past one or more other state tracts that I can check out.

Minnesota was probably the state that got the aspen band-wagon rolling. In the mid and late sixties grouse numbers soared to new heights, then dropped a little. Now, I'm told, they're climbing right back up—perhaps due to even more intensive aspen management. Wisconsin has gotten into aspen heavily as well. I talked with two Virginia hunters who claimed they bagged almost one hundred grouse during a two week stay in Wisconsin. Don't holler "Killers!" too loud. Limits are gener-ous; they could have bagged more.

Unfortunately, every state can't manage aspen like the three mentioned. It simply won't grow as well in other areas. How-ever, areas in the maritime provinces of Canada, Maine, the rest of New England, much of New York, and a lot of Pennsylvania and Ohio are capable of growing more aspen than they currently are. It's a matter of supply and demand—if more aspen is needed economically, more will be grown.

The reasons grouse favor aspen are many; but they need aspen in several different age classes. Clear-cutting huge two and three-thousand-acre tracts will not help. Grouse love to eat aspen buds, which grow on mature trees, in winter. This food is exceptionally high in protein, and it's always available, no matter how much snow covers the ground or how hard it's crusted. Grouse use the thick close-to-ground cover of recently harvested apsen for escape. The edges where insects hatch are usually ideal for nesting. Shortly after the young chicks emerge from the nest, this high protein food is critical to their future well-being.

In much of New England and the maritime provinces, grouse feed heavily on apples, especially in the early season. But grouse love apples no matter where they're found in North America. Any hunter seeing a tree laden with this fruit should work toward it, anticipating a flush. For this reason, I've always enjoyed hunting an old abandoned farm. The long-deceased proprietors invariably planted apple trees, and just as invari-ably, several of them will still be bearing fruit.

While the planted trees of the Mackintosh, Rome Beauty, Yellow Delicious and Winesap varieties have been productive, so are crab apple stands, where the twisted limbs and long, sharp thorns look eerie and foreboding. Grouse feed on the tiny green apples such stands produce, so enter without worry to your already tattered pants, ripped shirt, and scarred wrists.

Slashings, the name given to a forest that has recently been cut but the unused top limbs not removed, are top grouse habitats, too—especially in New England and throughout the Appalachians. But these slashings need to be in the right stage of development. If too high, they're past their prime, producing only a smattering of grouse flushes. The first year or so after cutting they are sometimes impenetrable, no matter how hearty the hunter. It's when they only seem impenetrable that slashings are best. This is the time when a bold grouser and his dog can have fun. They might not get many open shots, but they'll flush birds. When they do make one of those great shots, with the odds stacked completely against them, it's a moment to be printed indelibly in the memory, to recall time and time again. Slashings don't last long; after four or five years they're past their prime. Reverting farms last longer. Good grouse sport might last for several decades around one.

I mentioned grey dogwood briefly. Every grouse hunter should familiarize himself with this vegetation. In banner years it produces tremendous quantities of fruit, and grouse savor them. Grey dogwood bear no resemblance to the flowering dogwood that produces the white blossoms in the spring. But this latter tree produces a red berry that grouse love, too. Flowering dogwoods are often found on open sidehills. Grouse like to laze around them on sunny afternoons, gorging on the red berries. Not only are you likely to find birds there on such a day, the shooting is likely to be open.

A wild raspberry patch is another top grouse location. These low bushes usually bear fruit for the early season, after which grouse abandon them. I had good luck hunting such spots in late September with Henri Dorin, who guides upland hunters around his home in Quebec, just north of the Vermont border.

Grey dogwood.

Corners are one of my absolute favorite grouse spots. Some corners stand out like a sore thumb, particularly if open cover surrounds the thicket; but most productive corners don't stand out. They're subtle. This is particularly true around reverting farms, in recently timbered-over aspen country, slashings, etc. Time and new growth camouflage fence rows, old fields, rock fences, rail fences, and other such hot pockets. Sometimes we forget why they're there, or that they're there at all—but game birds don't forget. They gravitate to such perfect hiding and feeding grounds as surely as the compass needle gravitates to the north.

The key here is to constantly be looking for corners, and don't hesitate to alter your course a little when you see one. Be

Joe Cignetti retrieves a grouse that rocketed out of an edge and died in the opening.

keenly alert with mind and gun around these appealing havens. They'll produce action, perhaps more than any other specifically mentioned grouse area. Expect flushes to come from within the edge of the thicket, not on the more open side.

Sometimes grouse move into somewhat open cover to feed. Usually they do so only in good weather; a sunny afternoon is a time to expect such behavior. Remember that thick cover must be close at hand. I already mentioned how grouse sometimes move into red dogwood stands in this manner. Expect similar behavior around mature aspen trees when the birds want to feed on the buds.

Last season I was hunting back toward the pickup. It hadn't been a good flush day, but as I was walking through a stand of red dogwood I noted that there were tremendous numbers of red berries on these trees. I knew I should have been particularly keen at that moment, but I wanted to jot down a note on a pad in my breast pocket, indicating for future reference that grouse often move into open country to feed—and a sunny afternoon like this one was a perfect time to check out such a place—especially red dogwood. I stopped, pulled out my pen and pad, and hadn't written three words when a grouse thundered out only five feet away, offering an easy shot. I stood there helpless, the 20 between my legs, one hand holding a ball point pen, the other a paper pad. I flushed that grouse one more time on follow-up, but he'd already proven his competence. I couldn't get a shot.

The list of potential top grouse spots must include the tops of hollows. You've probably flushed plenty of grouse in such places and never realized that's what they were—tops of hollows. They don't have to be big hollows or steep hollows. Hollows of any kind will do. Around the upper portion, move your thumb a little closer to the safety. Like corners, many hollow tops are subtle, but start seeking them out. You'll note your flush rate increasing.

One year in Michigan I was having trouble finding grouse. Although I plowed excellent cover that had produced admirably the previous fall, the grouse simply weren't there. Nothing seemed unusual, but a gas station attendant passed on the clue. It had been one of the driest summers on record. Recent rains made the ground and vegetation seem normal, however. The grouse had been forced closer and closer to water during the drought. Evidently there was still plenty of food in such places, because they had not yet moved back to their regular haunts.

I dug out my county maps, found state land with lakes and ponds and swamps, and in an hour I was into grouse. It was that simple. The birds weren't around any old body of water; it had to be surrounded by a thicket. A frustrating two days was followed by a bonanza the rest of the week. In dry years don't forget that grouse need water.

Creek bottoms also produce in many areas, though not necessarily only in dry years. In mountain country, streams go far over their banks almost every spring. This causes some degree of devastation to the stream bank vegetation, bowling over some trees that provide cover and making room for the new growth that grouse love. While the surrounding mountain sides and mountain tops might be covered with maturing trees that grouse can't use for cover, the stream beds may be strewn with slash and fresh new growth that these birds thrive on.

Although I killed my first grouse in tall conifers, I've killed very few other birds in such places. Sometimes I drive a patch of pines, hoping for a chance to reflush. It seldom works. But hunting low pines can be most productive. The county where I live adjoins one that claims to be the Christmas tree capitol of the world. In these low pines I've enjoyed some great days.

Cultivated trees are out of the question. Not only are most posted against trespass, workers are in these plantations during hunting season, harvesting the trees prior to the arrival of the Christmas season. But there are thousands of acres of abandoned Christmas trees, too. Here the owners have found them too much trouble for too little profit, or perhaps the owners have died and the heirs didn't care for the hard work of pruning and harvesting. Once abandoned it doesn't take long before

a Christmas tree plantation becomes a grouse haven. Briars
and vines soon start weaving the edges of the tract, continu-
ously working their way toward the center. If hunted before
the pines grow too tall, such coverts can be particularly rewarding.

Paper and lumber companies often open their lands to
hunters—sometimes with welcome signs. These companies
usually manage their tracts intensively, and intensive forest
management is to the benefit of game, especially grouse. Find
out what companies own land in your area. A letter to their
PR department will result in a prompt answer and sometimes
they will even send a map.

Constantly searching for new cover is the key to consistent
success. Don't keep returning to an old favorite because it once
produced a memorable day—that's wasting valuable hunting
time. The habitat changes are subtle and not easily discerned;
but once cover grows too tall, it pays to look for a new haven.

However, once you locate a patch that's loaded with birds,
don't save it for next year. Pound a good spot without worry
to how many you kill—don't, however, bag more than the
daily limit. If the heavy cover is there, they'll be back next
season. However, don't hunt such a spot every day. The birds
will become too wary, maybe flushing the moment you slam
the car door. Once a week is enough.

6

Finding Woodcock

When I was a fledgling hunter, ready to reach out and experience my first out-of-state shooting adventure, my compatriot and I planned a trek to New Brunswick. Like most tyros, we didn't know much about woodcock. We also didn't even know that the wonderful maritime province we were planning to visit cradled perhaps the world's highest population of woodcock—at least at that time in history.

It was grouse we had in mind when we booked our hunt with Arlie Day, a guide who runs a fishing and hunting camp on the shores of Palfrey Lake near McAdam, New Brunswick. We must have looked skeptical on our evening of arrival as we listened while Arlie tried to take our minds off ruffs while he spun interesting tales of timberdoodle encounters.

Old time gun buffs will remember the name of Larry Koller. In the early sixties he was one of my favorite gun writers.

He had his own monthly magazine, which I believe was called *Guns and Hunting*. Among other things, Koller was an enthusiastic woodcock chaser. I wonder if he didn't have some sort of financial interest in Arlie's camp for he went there often. He was constantly trying to figure out the landlocked salmon in the Palfrey and Spednik Lake chain. At least that's what he did in the spring, sometimes into the summer. But in the fall Larry became enthralled with the plentiful woodcock in the nearby alder covers. Young and impressionable, I listened awe-struck as Arlie Day related exploits of Koller's skill with a scattergun. "He almost always uses a 28-gauge, and he almost never misses a bird!" That was just one of the quotes that has stayed with me through the years.

Except for a few farms, a fair share of crystal clear creeks and rivers, and a smattering of fish-filled lakes, New Brunswick is almost all alders—one massive woodcock cover from top to bottom, from side to side.

Arch Hulings was my shooting companion that trip. He toted a fairly new Browning Superposed in 12-gauge with 26½-inch barrels choked improved cylinder and modified. I had recently swapped a Black and Tan coon hound for the ordnance I cradled, a 12-gauge Parker V Grade with the unusual boring of 40 percent and over 70 percent—about cylinder or improved cylinder and full. Arlie Day claimed we were overgunned. "A 20s all ya' need for these little woodcock fellers." His was an American-made side-by-side, but I no longer recall the name of the manufacturer.

We tramped some dandy covers that first day. Arlie hadn't expected to hunt with tyros who could walk as far and as fast as Arch and I could. The next morning Arlie was the last one to crawl out of bed.

The limit was eight woodcock per day, plus four grouse. I don't think we ever limited out on the latter, but we always bagged a few, plus we had great luck with the tims. It was a hunt I'll long remember because of the outstanding success we enjoyed, and because Arlie had introduced us to what Frank

"Von" Woolner calls the "whistledoodle."

Not only did I learn a lot about the hunting of the twist-ing, twittering timberdoodle, I also found out a lot about where it resides on that trip. Alders were the key, and I've been pursuing this long-billed challenge in such tangles for years. Any reader who doesn't recognize alders when he sees them should learn to identify them.

Alders grow in rich, moist soil. Woodcock don't gravitate to alders because they like the way they look or because the bushes give them some special extra protection that others don't. These birds stay in alder tangles because earthworms thrive where alders thrive. As mentioned in an earlier chapter, the earthworm is the woodcock's primary food.

Alders do well along stream banks. A flat spot along the bank is often better than a sloping one. Many streams and rivers have wide, flat flood plains at major bends—a top place to encourage your belled, pointing dog and to load up your lightest upland ordnance.

Remember that a key to woodcock habitat is moisture. Worms thrive in moist, soft soil. If it's dry, hard, and caked, they won't be there. Even if worms were there, woodcock would not be able to get their beaks through the hard surface to catch them. Experienced woodcock hunters often know when a portion of the patch they are hunting is virtually prime for a flush. Underfoot there's a certain soft carpet feeling that makes it easier for tims to probe. While that feeling under-foot is soft, the ground does not give way so that the boots sink in. Every time you flush a woodcock next season, try to remember to take two more steps. You'll soon discover the feeling underfoot I'm trying to describe.

In some covers grouse and woodcock exist together. You'll normally find one and not the other, however. Hunting Quebec, north of Vermont, with guide Henri Dorin, we found the two birds living in harmony—at least in late September before the tims headed for warmer climes.

Here the cover was a mixture of tree and shrub species

Henri Dorin of Quebec and the author's yellow lab.

and, for woodcock, that always necessary soft carpet feeling underneath. On the afternoon of arrival my dogs were whining with enthusiasm, and my trigger finger was plagued with that certain itch. Henri had tasks he needed to attend to, but he suggested I walk across his pasture and hay field to the wood-lot beyond. "That patch was timbered-over a few years ago. You'll find partridge most anywhere, woodcock in the wet places."

Tim (short for Timberdoodle Tim) was the pointer I tried first. A short, hour and a half hunt produced plenty of action, with me missing several grouse but scoring on a brace of woodcock. Henri was justly proud of his little home cover when I returned to the farmhouse as the sun was glinting through the clouds to the west, turning them magnificent shades of red and purple.

We tried several covers the next day, and the best was still a mixture of low tree and shrub species. Here one couldn't find the endless expanses of alder that I had tramped in New Brunswick, but there were alders. They were interspersed with pine, cedar, tamarack, aspen, and birch—typical Canadian bush country.

The bush of Quebec and Ontario is usually a thick, low cover that is ideal for game like grouse and woodcock. Because of the short growing season, these trees and shrubs mature slowly. The result is that a cover can last a long time compared with the life of a bird habitat farther south. Remember the key to woodcock in the bush is wet ground.

Though most of my hunts in Michigan have been aimed at grouse, there have been many days when I've encountered ideal timberdoodle habitat and an abundance of long bills.

One day a couple of years ago I got into them with two dogs down, the brother and sister combo of Grouse Magic and Timberdoodle Tim. I was in a patch of aspen with a few other species mixed in. From the road it looked like most of the other aspen patches I had been hunting and finding grouse in that October. If there was any difference, it was that these trees and shrubs were a little higher. If the ground was more moist or softer under foot, I don't remember it.

Magic racked up tight next to a little clump of grey dogwood, and I walked in expecting the roaring and speedy departure of a grouse. Instead a woodcock came helicoptering up, in slow motion compared to ruff. I overswung with both barrels, and a second later the bird was parachuting back into the cover.

Magic found that one for the second time. I was carrying my custom Mario Beschi 20-gauge side-by-side that day. It had too much drop, so I tended to shoot under rising birds. Compensating for the low-shooting tendency on that flush, I sent him toppling. Both dogs broke point, trying to beat one another to the find. Tim beat Magic by a whisker and pranced back proud as Hollywood Henderson after the runback of an interception. He was so happy he looked like he could have spiked it.

Soon Tim was on point, and I cautioned Magic with a "whoa" as she worked in. I thought maybe she wouldn't see her brother in time. Again I missed on the first flush, but the 'doodle didn't fly far. I saw him dive back into the aspen ahead. I pocketed four woodcock with those two staunch dogs in a matter of minutes, and I hadn't marched more than a couple hundred yards from my vehicle. Feeling sure there were more birds ahead, I heeled the young duo back to the pickup and exchanged them for my yellow lab, Honey. He needed some work.

Honey sniffed a long bill before we went very far into that cover, and I connected with the little side-by-side with 24-inch barrels. They were choked true cylinder and improved, which I consider ideal for woodcock. I've since cured the problem of too much drop by installing a Variable Pad from Meadow Industries, Box 92, Meadow Lands, PA 15347. This pad is incomparably better than the lace-on variety that has been in vogue for years. The Variable Pad attaches to the butt stock with velcro fasteners, so there's no slippage, a problem I always encountered with the lace-on pads. The Variable Pad is supplied with six or seven different thicknesses of interchangeable spacers, which can be used alone or in tandem. These fit underneath the stretchable, leather-like Naugahyde pad. By building mine up to .355 inches, I have that handy little 20 shooting right where it should.

But back to Michigan. The point I wanted to make was that when the timberdoodle hunter can encounter just the

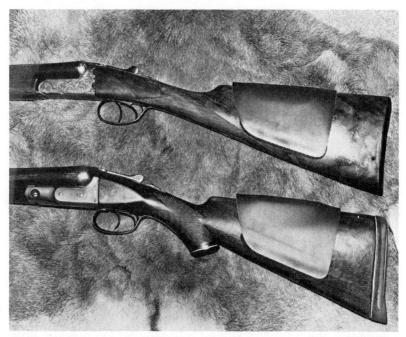

On top, the author's 20-gauge Mario Beschi custom. Below, a Parker 12. Both are fitted with Variable Pads.

right aspen, he may be in for some great action. I'm certain I lucked into a little flight of woodcock during that short hunt just described. Native birds are seldom so concentrated.

On another occasion John Kriz, wildlife biologist with the Pennsylvania Game Commission, introduced me to some of his aspen covers in Erie County, Pennsylvania. We were into birds immediately at the first patch we tried, a young stand of aspen only a little more than head high. It was plagued with clinging briars, so thick that I marveled how the woodcock could flush through them—but they did. We also had young Andy Martin along that day. It was his first woodcock hunt.

My main dog that year was Star, the hard driving pointer who was then in her prime. I swear she made her first point before we were even into the cover. We bagged seven or eight tims that morning, though Andy hadn't scored. Young aspen was the main cover species. Naturally, there were some other species, but aspen—and briars—were the keys to our success.

We stopped for a bite at a luncheon counter in Albion, where we met another long-bill enthusiast. He wasn't enjoying much success and had flushed only a single bird all morning, while we were enjoying a seemingly endless parade of flushes. I'll never forget what he said to us as he was parting. "I can't understand it. I'm hunting the same aspen covers that I have for years. But every season there are fewer birds in them. I can't understand it."

We climbed into my vehicle and headed for another hot-spot. John Kriz's comment was, "Why can't hunters realize that bird covers have a life and a death? As long as that guy keeps returning to old places, he's going to be disappointed. I wanted to tell him to seek out younger aspen stands, but I knew he wouldn't listen."

I hunt woodcock in many different covers over the course of a season, but my bread and butter spots are the flood plains of flood control dams. While alders predominate on most of them, there are also crabs, aspen, hawthorn, willow, etc.

I have one favorite spot which I won't name; Scott Harrison has another. We sometimes scour my favorite opening day, his on the second day. Alders are especially prevalent on the flood plain he loves. We've had so many memorable hunts at both that it's difficult to recall which one is most appropriate for illustrative purposes in this chapter.

That flood plain is one of many where the hunter keeps working in and out of perfect and less than perfect cover. We usually walk down an old tram past a row of wildflowers, entering the patch where the alders begin. Here the ground growth is minimal, also a necessity when one expects to find woodcock in abundance. Steve Liscinsky, game biologist in Pennsylvania who wrote the booklet *The American Woodcock in Pennsylvania*, determined scientifically that grass should cover about 25 percent of the ground in ideal woodcock cover. If there is more grass than that, birds can't move around unencumbered. If there is less than 25 percent, the supply of worms in the ground won't be high.

At Scott's favorite flood plain, the number of woodcock encountered varies in direct proportion to the amount of vegetation at ground level. There are some good-looking spots, but they simply have too much grass underfoot. Here we seldom find a bird. But as soon as we enter alders where the grass begins to thin out, we get ready for the twitter of wings. At that flood plain, the variation in grass cover shows how dependent woodcock are on the right ground-level vegetative condition.

Walt Lesser, biologist with the West Virginia Department of Natural Resources, was good enough to show me one of his prime covers in the Canaan Valley, famous woodcock hotspot in the high West Virginia mountains that the birds utilize on their route to the south. The key here was the cattle grazing. One of Walt's favorite spots was a dense thicket of alders and wild spirea. The alders were tough to penetrate, and in places the spirea was impossible.

Star was again in her prime that year. I was running another pointer, too, Trixie. She wasn't half the dog Star was, but she had a good day or two in West Virginia that year. I limited out the first afternoon and the following morning. There were several reasons for my success.

One reason was the young spirea that was two to four feet high. It was sort of sinful to shoot woodcock flushing out of this low brush, for they were easy marks with no vegetation around them. There were more than a few birds in this low spirea. The second reason was the cattle, or more to the point, the places where they had tramped down the vegetation as they moved about grazing. These tramped-over areas were on the ground level so woodcock could have the room to move around that they always require, yet the canopy above of alder branches and leaves gave them the security from flying predators that they also need.

For the last two years I've been returning to a little cover in Clarion County, Pennsylvania, a patch that I had been passing up for several seasons. It takes an hour and a half to get there, and I had been finding plenty of birds closer to home. It's a small cover, and I don't know any others close to it. I found it originally because a close friend, though not a woodcock hunter, had a deer camp right across the dirt road. He heard shooting one fall, investigated, and found a briar-ripped hunter and a shorthair. My friend told me that the guy had been chasing woodcock. I pulled out a piece of paper and pencil and immediately mapped out directions. It's been a dreamy little haven. Two years ago, when I returned after missing several seasons, I pocketed a quintet of long bills in only thirty minutes. Last season it only took about thirty-five minutes, but I chased a grouse on a reflush (pocketed him, too).

This patch is a perfect mixture with aspen in several stages of growth, alders, hawthorn, and spirea. It appears that the place is an abandoned farm. The higher cover, which was so bird filled six or seven years ago, doesn't produce much any more. These days woodcock are concentrating in the lower vegetation that is emerging on the outer perimeter of the higher cover. Any time one can find such habitat on a reverting farm, it's likely to contain plenty of game, notably woodcock. On the other side, there's a new hunting camp almost in the center of the covert, so it's doomed. Someday soon it will be off limits.

Bob Parlaman has been good enough to show me some of his favorite haunts in southern Crawford County. Along the migration route of woodcock flying south, a hunter can find great concentrations of birds in these aspen patches if he hits it right. As in other areas of northwestern Pennsylvania, aspen predominates, although top covers are often characterized by some degree of mixture of young tree and shrub species. Parlaman spent his working career with the Pennsylvania Game Commission, and he knows bird cover in his bailiwick better than anyone I've ever been with in that area. He has a keen eye for the habitat woodcock choose, and he drove the back roads

Brace of woodcock, bird gun, and the woodcocks' "white splash" calling card between the birds. Fresh droppings are a sure indication that woodcock are nearby.

twelve months out of the year on his job. The fact that he continually spotted bird country from the road added to his game bag in October.

Being able to recognize cover from the road is very important, more so with woodcock than with grouse. As a rule, woodcock covers are smaller. It's not unusual to turn the dogs loose in a one-acre patch. It will only take a matter of minutes to check it out, to see if any birds are in residence or not. Even if one finds a bird or two, it'll take only a half an hour to thoroughly hunt such a tiny spot. Then it's on to another.

Hunting in this manner requires five to ten little patches to make a full days hunt. Hunting close to old country dirt roads is a necessity, for it's not worth a one hour walk back into a smallish haven, merely to see if there might be a bird or two gobbling worms. Thus there is the necessity of being able to spot potential bird havens from the vehicle. What do you look for?

Try to avoid traveling on hard roads when checking. Usually there are too many dwellings close by, making shooting unsafe. There's also an added danger to bird dogs because of the increased traffic that travels at higher speeds. Concentrate looking along creeks, marshes, lakes, and reservoirs that are bordered by dirt roads. Look for rather low vegetation in these areas. Being able to identify certain tree and shrub species like aspen, alder, crab apple, hawthorn, spirea, etc., makes spotting potential hotspots easy. Finally, don't forget to have a notebook and/or a county map along to make a permanent record of your findings.

Sometimes the twisting, twittering, winged timberdoodle is an anomaly. The Fish and Wildlife Service claims the harvest is dropping though they admit the reduction in take has been small. Yet my bag seems to get bigger every fall, while I seem to spend fewer hours pursuing them. At the same time, some covers are eliminated by new homes, development, and other results of population growth. Covers peak out and a maturing timber stage takes over, offering little prospect for the long bill's future. Still, I find more covers than I can hunt in a season, and I meet others who also have no trouble. While filling a limit of two grouse per day occurs with a disturbing degree of scarcity in my home covers, filling with five tims is seldom difficult.

Al Schwartz and his setter, plus a few woodcock he bagged. Al was instrumental in creating the Pennsylvania Grouse Association, now a part of the Ruffed Grouse Society.

7

Dogs For Grouse Hunting

I've already made my case concerning the different techniques required to hunt grouse as opposed to woodcock and explained the subtle differences in their habitat. While writers have erroneously talked about "grouse and woodcock" hunters, assuming each bird was hunted by similar methods, they've talked about "grouse and woodcock dogs," making similar assumptions. My view is that there are significant differences in top grouse and top woodcock dogs. Only canines capable of changing their style of hunting are capable of falling into the category of top "grouse and woodcock dogs".

The first bird dog I ever owned was a German shorthair, Radar. He was precocious. By the time he was six months old, he'd had fifty birds killed in his whereabouts. Most were woodcock, a few were grouse. Over his lifetime he spent maybe three or four times as many hours in pursuit of grouse, but he

never pointed one dead to rights. In contrast, he was the sharp-
est woodcock campaigner I've ever seen or owned. What made
him better at one than the other?

Primarily it was the way he hunted. He didn't go about
the task slow, but he was thorough. He didn't quarter in classic
fashion, but he left little cover unsmelled. When he winded a
long bill he became cautious, kept creeping closer—but so, so
carefully—until he had the tim pinned sometimes literally
right under his nose. He bumped very few woodcock into the
air, either accidentally or on purpose. Although he wasn't run
with other dogs often, he was never out-birded. On several
hunts he made every point, while his bracemate did nothing
the entire hunt but play second fiddle, backing.

But in the grouse woods Radar was a sorry case. I did,
however, shoot grouse over him. When braced with another
grouse dog, Radar played second fiddle while his bracemate
encountered scent before he did. When Radar smelled grouse
on his own, he tried to handle them the same way he handled
a woodcock. He never learned to change his hunting style.
He'd slow or stop when he got a whiff, then ease in close.
Though long bills will stand for such shenanigans, this tactic is
guaranteed to send ruffed grouse into the air. They are extremely sensitive to the approach of dog or man, and in the last
ten years the birds in my local haunts have become even more
wary, flushing for even less reason, flushing even farther
ahead. While training or buying a good woodcock dog is relatively easy, the outstanding grouse dog is tough to find.

The first great grouse dog I ever saw in action was Lawrence Cignetti's Nuc, short for Nuclear. A pointer directly out
of national champion Wayriel Allegheny Sport, Nuc was of
medium size, lanky though not skinny. He flowed through a
thicket, he didn't run. His range wasn't overly wide (in the
fifty-yard to one-hundred-fifty-yard range) unless he wasn't
finding any grouse. Then he had no compunctions about strik-
ing out like a treeing walker rambling for coon scent. Nuc didn't
come back under such circumstances. He found and pointed a

grouse, and it was up to you to find him. Just watching Nuc run was as thrilling as seeing him on point. He had that flair about him much as great people do, a magnetism that was awe-inspiring.

I was lucky to hunt behind that dog a lot, and he never ceased to amaze me. But I wonder if he'd have been as good with today's more wary grouse. I wonder if his fast tendencies and fair range would have flushed a lot more birds today than they did back then. Somehow I think Nuc was one of the last, great, hard-driving grouse dogs, for I think today's bird, especially in areas that are heavily hunted, requires a dog with slightly different traits.

There's one trait I insist on, no matter what type of hunting canine we're talking about, and that's hunting desire. Still, I have no use for a dog with hunting desire that takes him over the ridge or into the next county. I want that hunting desire tempered with good sense and a desire to produce for me, not for himself—important though admittedly academic.

My ideal grouse dog wears a bell that never goes out of hearing, but I still see him often, no matter how thick the cover. He checks back to see where I am. I don't say a word to encourage him back. Sometimes he stops to listen. I indicate where I am by continuing to walk so the dog can hear me, or by giving a low whistle. If he's out of sight for more than a minute, I head for the spot where I heard the bell last—he's probably on point.

Star, a female pointer now in old age, has undoubtedly been my best bird dog yet; but she is not a good dead-bird finder, nor does she retrieve. This is an important grouse dog trait. Consequently, Star was never the complete bird dog since she showed so little interest in zeroing in on a dead or wounded grouse. Once the bird was down she wanted to find another live one. That was the hunting challenge to her.

With most feather finders, the desire to hunt dead is coupled with the desire to retrieve, although good retrievers aren't necessarily top dead-bird finders. I didn't have Star as a

Grouse Magic retrieves.

pup. I bought her as a started dog almost two years old. If I had the opportunity to work with her as a youngster, I think I could have increased her interest in searching for dead birds.

The way to accomplish that task is with pigeons. There are usually neighborhood kids around looking for extra money who will live trap pigeons, but dead ones are almost as useful for this purpose. If I have live birds I spin the pigeon to sleep, get the dog out, and have a companion work the pup on a check cord. Hopefully the dog will point, I'll flush the pigeon, then kill it. The check cord keeps him in close to hunt dead, though when young, few pups reach out.

With dead pigeons, start by tossing them out into a close-cropped field. When the dog gets the hang of that, pitch the dead pigeons into a heavy grass field. They'll have to use their noses in addition to their eyes for this. All the time they're looking, encourage them with enthusiastic repetitions of "Dead bird. Dead bird."

On the next outing, flip the pigeon out when the dog isn't looking. Then encourage the dog into the area with "Dead bird. Dead bird." Act like you would if a real grouse was down, moving into the area yourself, directing the dog to the approximate location with a wave of the hand.

Most any potlicker will run to where a bird falls if it happens in plain view. But many grouse that are downed the dog never sees. That's why the latter, basic retrieving technique I've recommended is so important.

Should a grouse dog be steady to wing and shot? There's no necessity, but it is a training refinement that I enjoy seeing. My dogs are trained to hold, but they break on occasion. I seldom get upset when they do. I don't participate in field trials any more. When I did, I insisted my dogs be steady, because breaking would automatically throw them out of any trial. It has been my experience that a dog who is trained steady to wing and shot is more dependable when he's on his game. Such a dog will have less of a tendency to creep forward and startle a wary grouse. A perfectly steady dog knows that flushing the bird prematurely results in discipline.

Spinning a pigeon to sleep during training session.

Many claim they want their dogs to break immediately to the flush so they reach the downed bird quicker, reasoning that fewer will escape. Once the bird's down, he's not going to get away. With few exceptions these hunters are unwilling to go to the trouble to make their dogs rock steady, or they don't know how.

On a quail hunt in Mississippi a few years ago, I hunted with a crackerjack pointer. He wasn't the field-trial type. He simply found the birds—all of them. It didn't matter that he was older and past his prime, or that his two bracemates were younger and racier. The next day I hunted with an excellent female, she out of the Kansas Wind, a former national champion. I found out that these two dogs had been mated, and the owner still had two pups left. I bought them both on the spot.

Grouse Magic on point.

The results were Timberdoodle Tim and Grouse Magic, a brother and sister duo I've been trying to make into grouse dogs. Making them suitable for woodcock hunting has been no problem. I think Magic is going to make a superb grouse dog as she gains more experience. This past season she had one great day, pointing grouse solidly more than a dozen times. I've never seen any bird dog do better, and I've walked behind some dan-

Grouse Magic and Timberdoodle Tim.

dies. Admittedly, it was a fortunate day for her. The grouse were holding, but she still did it. I think the way I've tried to train her has been instrumental to her adapting so well.

While her mother and father both possessed tremendous hunting desire, they tempered it with common sense. I selected my pups from top parents. Everyone should. I feel this is an extremely important point.

Magic never was a wide ranger, and I've never encouraged her to romp. Still she ranges plenty, so I restrict her—with discipline if she persists in staying out of sight for long. Fortunately I don't have to do that often. Her natural range, coupled with a desire to hunt for me (and a few switchings), keep her much closer than Cignetti's Nuclear stayed, discussed at the beginning of this chapter.

By keeping the dog in closer I've been aware of more wild flushing grouse—flushes I would never have known occurred if the dog ranged slightly farther because I'd never have seen or heard them. In many instances I've been able to follow up such flushes and score. On a few occasions the dog has been close enough that I've seen her bump a grouse. When that's happened, I've bumped her. If she had been a wider ranger, I'd never have known anything wrong took place, and the dog wouldn't have learned as quickly that bumping was wrong.

I've worked with her on pigeons from the start, so she's an enthusiastic dead-bird finder. She'll scurry around the fall area until she finds what she's looking for, and she's exceedingly earnest while doing so.

Wing-tipped or well-hit, but not dead, grouse are quick to crawl under something. In the places where these birds live, there's always a lot to crawl under. This habitat condition is the primary reason why grouse dogs should be ardent dead-bird finders. Many grouse disappear as the shot is taken. By pausing briefly after every such shot, the sportsman will often be able to hear an unseen, dead bird hit the ground—but not always.

Many other grouse that we shoot at get belted with several

pellets, yet show no sign of being injured before disappearing, still on good wings. It pays to follow up every grouse anyway, but particularly those where you know the shot felt right though the bird didn't fall. A thorough retriever that will stay in close under this condition will put several more birds in your coat every season.

All of which brings up another point. A fairly close-working dog, like I have tried to describe in Magic, will point more grouse when trying to follow them up. Because the hunter marks the departing flight of the grouse visually, he often has an excellent idea where to find it—a tremendous advantage over the dog. The canine that works in more reasonable range during a follow-up will go to that bird and point it because such a dog naturally works ahead of the hunter's path. A wider ranger might not be inclined to do that.

It's important that no dog travel faster than his nose permits. The better his olfactory powers, the faster he can go. But I've seen many a dog fail time after time on grouse because he traveled at too fast a pace for his nose, flushing grouse after grouse, perhaps stopping to flush—mannerly but frustrating. Although it's possible to restrict a dog's range, it's much tougher to restrict his speed. Consequently, the need for a top nose can never be over-stressed. A dog with a top nose and average speed will still point birds. A dog with an average nose and top speed ends up getting his butt switched repeatedly.

After Radar, all my experience with dogs that I've owned has been with pointers and English setters. However, I did spend two years training bird dogs professionally. During that period I had the opportunity to work with lots of pointers and setters, several other shorthairs, brittanies, and griffons. I've had the opportunity to hunt over other pointing dogs—vizslas and wirehaired vizslas (now called "the Uplander" by an enterprising kennel).

I know there are some good brittanies around. I'm not being sarcastic when I say I've only seen one of them. Evidently I've been a victim of circumstance and always been in the wrong place at the wrong time. A recent correspondent told me about an old brittany he had the good privilege to hunt with in Maine's Washington County last season. This aging bitch did everything but drive the car, she was that smart and that responsive to her owner's wishes.

My problem with brittanies has been that I've been unable to get them to point. The ones I trained always wanted to sneak in and flush the bird. My training methods are evidently at odds with this breed's make-up. Of course, I know many a bird hunter who has thrown his hands up, frustrated with the hard-headedness of the pointer, the breed with which I've had my best luck.

I have had success with German shorthairs, although I firmly believe they're potentially better suited to woodcock than grouse. They're thorough, have excellent noses, an overriding desire to search dead and retrieve, and they point well, albeit not with the staunchness of the typical pointer or setter. You can't beat these latter two when it comes to degree of pointing instinct.

But shorthairs and brittanies have become quite popular, though I wonder if there's not a trend back to pointers and setters of late. More and more new grouse hunters (and woodcock hunters, too) are realizing how beneficial an appreciable amount of white can be on a dog. Heavily ticked or all liver-colored shorthairs are beautiful to the eye, but they're difficult to see in the thicket, especially once they're on point.

With few exceptions, pointers, English setters, and brittanies have enough white coloring in their coats that they are easy to see. Within the last ten years some shorthair breeders have been attempting to get more white into their dogs. Some claim there's been an influx of pointer blood to accomplish this. The important thing for a grouse hunter looking for a German shorthair to grace his kennel is that there are now dogs available with plenty of white on their coat from which to choose.

Although the taking of a grouse that has flushed from in

Springer spaniels make excellent grouse dogs.

front of a steady point is the supreme thrill in the entire world to me, I do use a flush dog occasionally. During my years as a professional trainer I worked with several labs, a golden, and two springer spaniels. Today a yellow lab occupies one of my kennel runs, so he gets his chance in grouse and woodcock cover when my pointers are worn out.

Though grouse and woodcock are the game birds I pursue with a fervor, when I pursue doves, pheasants, and waterfowl in search of story material, the yellow lab has been most useful. A ham in front of the camera, he'll hold pheasants, grouse, ducks, woodcock, doves, etc., for roll after exposed roll. By being around in grouse and woodcock season, he gets his chance to prove added worth.

Little training is required before one of these flush dogs can produce feathers. Lab, golden, or springer, they love hunting, and they know how to go about the task. Normally close-workers, what they flush is within shooting range, though this is not always the case before the leaves fall. Of course, under those conditions even a well-pointed bird might escape without a shot being fired.

I recommend going through the pigeon-retrieving training exercises described earlier. This will whet a flusher's taste for searching dead, and with labs, goldens, or springers, their retrieving instincts take little whetting.

It's also important to restrict their range. They tend to work too far out after they've had a decent taste of what hunting is all about. This is usually the result of their hard hunting desire, but it's easily tempered since they also have an over-riding desire to please the person who feeds them.

It's impossible not to get attached to a hunting dog. They all have their lovable ways, individual antics, and even the worst of the lot produces an indelible memory on the rare occasion. It's not easy to cut the cord with a dog that is not suitable —but this is the only sensible solution to a seemingly insolvable problem.

Retrievers like this yellow lab can make very good grouse dogs.

I have given up on many dogs. Even when I was training professionally, I restricted my fees when I thought I was incapable of making significant improvement on any individual. I usually knew whether or not I could make headway within a week. With my own young dogs I have been willing to take more time. Some of the questionable ones I hoped would make it, while I didn't have any confidence in others. Few of either ever did much. I knew great pups were going to make great dogs the first time I saw them in action. Fortunately I've had the good sense to give away dogs that were going to waste my time.

This isn't meant to claim that every dog I've ever kept has been a great one on grouse. Far from it. But if a dog is totally unsuitable, what's the sense in butting your head against a stone wall for the next decade? It has never been easy to part with any canine that has graced my backyard kennel, but I know I always did the right thing in giving it up.

Giving away an unsuitable dog will give you the opportunity to try a new pup, or a new breed, or a new partly or fully trained dog. Doing so can result in grouse hunting fulfillment, while keeping a dog that you know won't ever work out can only result in total frustration.

8

Dogs For
Woodcock Hunting

A grouse dog is a rare jewel, a diamond in the rough. A woodcock dog is considerably more common and as plentiful as rhinestones. I hope you'll now permit me some divergence—intended to make a point. (No pun intended.)

Up until two years ago I had been a haphazard skeet shooter. I'd go hot and cold, firing a couple of rounds in the off season, then take a six month layoff. But two summers ago the skeet bug bit me good, and I started shooting regularly during spring and summer, sometimes shooting four rounds (one hundred shells) on fall Sundays (a non-hunting day in my home state).

Skeet is an excellent game for a gunner who has hunting experience and thinks he's a better than average shot. He soon learns that he's not so hot. More than anything else, skeet teaches gun swing. Although many chances at grouse and woodcock are straightaways, many are quartering or full-crossing shots, where fast swings are imperative. I recommend concentrated skeet shooting to any upland enthusiast. Of course, the game was originally developed by a small group of grouse hunters who wanted to improve their technique. If you are not interested in competitive skeet, it will pay dividends to keep the gun down when calling for the target, thus simulating field conditions more closely. Actually, skeet was originally shot from the gun-down position.

But this game has taught me more than swing alone. I also learned the importance of gun mounting, especially nestling the stock's comb just right against my cheek. Prior to this concentrated practice I'm certain I often fired at both grouse and woodcock with the gun hardly touching my cheek, if at all.

I was carrying my custom-made Mario Beschi that first fall after considerable skeet shooting. It had more than the normal amount of drop in the stock, 24-inch barrels choked

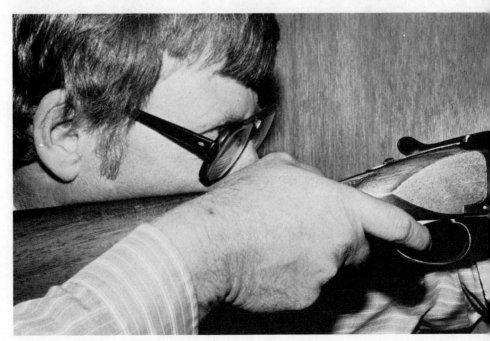

Learn to cheek the shotgun solidly.

true cylinder and improved. The fore-end was a splinter. The grip was straight, sometimes referred to as English. During the week prior to Pennsylvania's opening day, I was in Michigan with that Mario Beschi, and shooting poorly—all because the shotgun had too much drop. I was continually shooting under those feathered targets.

So what does all this have to do with woodcock dogs? I'm getting to it. It was a frustrating week in Michigan. By still using that Italian custom on opening day in Pennsylvania, I was able to encounter an inordinate number of game contacts with Magic, my young three year old. Of course, the plentiful game contacts occurred because I missed so damned often. It took a lot of points, flushes, and shots before I was finally able to limit out. That day Magic performed so many of the tasks for which woodcock dogs are often called upon, and she performed them admirably.

It was a damp morning, though not raining. The vegetation was saturated. Scenting conditions must have been excellent. Less than fifteen minutes past legal shooting light I turned Magic loose. One and a half hours later I had twelve empties in my pocket, had seen twenty woodcock in the air, and Magic had produced seven solid points. I've retrieved all this information from my gunning log. The first four words after the date are, "Best Opening Day Ever!"

Magic did her wind sprints up and down the pipeline I always use to make my entrance into that flood-plain thicket. Then I directed her into the right side of the patch with a hand signal, following right behind. The cover was mainly alder, with a smattering of crab apple, grey dogwood, and several other low tree and shrub species.

Under foot, the dank earth felt just right, soft and wet, but not boggy. I get a similar feeling walking on an extra-deep pile or long, shag carpet. Magic was flashing in and out of sight often, racing because it was early and her vim and vigor level was high. Her bell was tinkling first on my left, then ahead, then on my right, then she'd flash briefly into view again.

I was anticipating either a wild flush or the bell to stop at any moment, so the side-by-side was at the port arms ready. Magic had just streaked into sight ahead when she whiffed the first game. A tiny step-across creek cut down through the little alder stand there, and Magic's front paws were in the run, her back legs up on the bank. Her head was cocked to the right—upstream. I couldn't help smiling at the odd position, but I didn't savor the sight long, anxious to get the first bird up and then promptly back on the ground. I had no trouble accomplishing the former, but my shotgun's fit was at odds with helping me accomplish the latter—a roundabout way of saying I missed.

Undaunted, Magic didn't look back my way with a scolding smirk when I released her with "All right." She was still excited about finding tims. In short order she was locked again. I had a good line in the direction the first doodle had taken, and even though Magic was spirited and didn't have her edge off yet, I was able to control her with low voice commands, keeping her perfectly directed to the area the tim had taken.

This time she struck a more classic pose—tail high, body erect, right fore leg drawn up, her whole being granite-like. I failed to put the classic finish to that picture, because I missed again. This time the bird presented a reasonable shot, vaulting from the edge of the opening where he had landed, quartering away at a forty-five-degree angle from right to left. Evidently I slapped the custom stock too tightly against my cheek (lots of practice on the skeet field) and directed the shot charge some distance underneath that brown feathered helicopter.

On the next point I found Magic in thick crabs after looking for almost five minutes. I love a dog that can be depended upon to not budge for a long period. I should have been listening more attentively to her bell, because she was less than thirty yards away when the clanging went silent. It's just as important for the dog's master to be constantly aware of the bell as it is for the dog to be staunch—if they expect to cooperate to mutual benefit.

A bell on the dog's collar helps the hunter keep track of the dog.

This one drilled up above the crabs, and I loosed the one ounce of 8s just as the bird reached the apex of its upward flight, but again the pellets failed to connect. I gritted my teeth, turned the dog loose, and followed in the path that critter had taken.

This time the woodcock fortunately landed in a somewhat different patch of cover; it was much lower. The bird pitched off only a few feet above ground just as Magic skidded into a point in the mud. I got lucky and dumped that one, probably because it was quartering away with no upward angle.

Magic broke the half-point she had made, raced to the fall, and scooped up the first bird of the day. She pranced back, showing her elation once by tossing it several inches into the air; then she picked it up again, clutching it softly, not harming a feather, which is her custom. Sometimes she drops the bird part way back and saunters off to locate another, but only if it is stone dead and only if she sees me first.

While the dog's edge now seemed worn down a bit, she still went about her task with purpose—fast paced, but methodically sniffing every little nook and cranny. She checked me often by stopping, her bell going silent. I'd give a low whistle and it would start again. If it didn't, I knew I had to look for her, for she'd be on point. Of course, no amount of whistling or calling could persuade her to break.

The next opportunity was a bird I flushed on my own as I bent over low, trying to force my way through a particularly thick stand of young, low alders. I quickly swung the always ready lightweight into action, only to miss with both tubes. As I listened to the woodcock twittering his departure, my temper was smoking just like the choke ends of my 20.

Magic, on hearing the double fusillade, was soon in the vicinity, scurrying and sniffing where the quarry had just departed. She locked tight where the bird had taken off, but I turned my back on her, urging, "Come on, lame brain. He's gone." At which time yet another tim came up with his wings all atwitter. I turned in time to get the safety off and get the little side-by-side almost to my shoulder, but he was gone before I could put the finishing touches to my act. The lesson? Always believe your dog, especially when you're disgusted with yourself.

The next bird was even more exasperating. Magic nailed it in a patch of cover that almost never fails to hold a tim. But I couldn't get it to flush. Finally I released the dog with a cautious, "All right. Easy now." With my shotgun barrels angled skyward, both hands caressed the stock, the butt tucked against the right side of my chest and under my right arm, my thumb toying with the safety button.

Magic eased forward, tail now swishing fast, head moving from side to side, nostrils pulsating as they probed the air for a dab of scent. Another point. But it, too, was not productive. So I released her again with caution, still maintaining the tight grip on my 20. Both a third and fourth point were unproductive. All the while my blood was coming closer and closer to the boiling point and my adrenalin was flowing. I could feel my heart throbbing in my chest. We had a runner here, and Magic was doing a superb job. I wanted to reward her valiant effort.

On the fifth point, she finally had the strong-legged bird pinned. It was at least thirty yards from where she had first located it—a magnificent performance. I made the improper salute, the 20 belching both tubes to futile avail. This time Magic held her ground with perfect manners, but rolled her eyes back at me. I swear there was disgust on her face.

"Sorry girl," was the best I could offer in the way of apologies. I moved off into the tight canopied cover with my head a little lower after that display.

By noon there had simply been so many birds and Magic had performed so well that I limited out with my quintet of long bills. I was now convinced that the blame on my inept shooting rested with the too-much-drop stock, but I didn't have sense enough to change before the next hunting day.

It was Star who starred in the next canine role. I was still the straight man in the act, performing on the second day to the high standards of missing that I had attained on the season opener.

I tried a new tract, for I seldom hunt a woodcock cover twice during the same year, never on successive days. In younger years, Star was far wider ranging than Magic, but the seasons have wound her springs down appreciably. She's still aggressive and energetic, covering more ground at a faster pace than someone knowing her age would expect. At the start of that second day I had to hack her a little, curbing her rambunctious attitude; but when she got down to business, I didn't

Star on point.

have to speak often to keep her range reasonable. When hunting woodcock I insist that the dogs stay in closer than in the grouse woods.

The dog was in sight when she rammed into the first woodcock. The cover consisted of thick, small clumps of vegetation with open ground between. There was a tiny tract of aspen, another of alders, several very small clumps of grey dogwood, plus one or two Viburnums that I can't identify scientifically. Star wasn't far away, and it was easy to spot her regularly because of the many openings.

Typical for her, Star had her head low to the ground, the bottom of her chin almost touching the few leaves that had fallen. Reacting crisply and without thought to which shotgun I had in my hand, I kicked the vegetation ahead of Star, flushed a twitterer, and directed the shot charge perfectly, even though the critter jinked right at the last instant. I was quick enough to stay with him for that maneuver. Or was it that the pattern was simply open enough to compensate?

The first bird in the day brought a smile to both my face and soul. Star, who hadn't seen the flush, held until I released her with my "All right." She feathered forward, tail knocking vegetation this way and that, then pointed dead. Though she seldom picks up a bird, except to chomp down hard several times, she often points dead ones—an important trait for a non-retriever or a hard-mouthed canine.

She was smart enough to force her way into the thickest part of a little clump of cover minutes later. Here she found what she was looking for—the dank scent of long bill. And they are dank smelling. Put a dead bird up to your nose some day and breathe in deeply. Though some feel woodcock have more scent than other game birds, I don't. I believe I can smell grouse easier than I can smell woodcock. Grouse also smell more appealing than tims.

Star held perfectly while I circled the little clump of cover, another important trait for a good 'doodle dog. But the wood-cock had its tactics all worked out. When the bird found I was trying to head it off at the pass, it launched in the opposite direc-tion, a course that took it through all manner of leaves and branches. I could hear it having difficulty getting through, but I couldn't see it. It appeared briefly as it topped the branches, but then it disappeared. As it did, I loosed a shot in despera-tion, without hope of connecting. I listened for a couple of seconds but didn't hear the bird fall. Just as importantly, per-haps, I didn't hear wings twittering on, either.

Star isn't one who likes to stay in close after a point and some shooting. The odor and the noise seem to turn her half-berserk. Unless her energy is curbed at such times she may take off in a race that doesn't bring her back to the point of action for ten minutes. But I knew we had to check for that bird, so I scolded sternly, not once but several times, all the while encour-aging her to search dead in the thicket where the tim had dis-appeared. She almost got away on me once, but when she swung in close again, she caught a whiff and locked solidly—pointing dead for the second time.

Two shots—two woodcock. Maybe this Mario Beschi would do after all. And that last shot had been as difficult and quick as any I've ever made.

But then my shooting started falling apart. I flushed thirty woodcock that morning, eventually limiting out, but I made up my mind I would change guns prior to my next outing. The fact that I missed so often only meant more opportunities for Star that day. We reflushed a lot of birds, and she pointed less than half of the thirty we did get into the air, but, still, that's a premier performance.

The next day I was behind Magic again, hunting in Erie County. The familiar Franchi 20-gauge autoloader was cradled in the port arms, however. I went to the same cover referred to in chapter 7, the one I hunted with Rich Drury, the one that is so difficult to reach due to the thick bog that must be traversed before one can reach the top spot.

Magic was her stellar self, and, as my gunning log indicates, my performance improved considerably. I went five for six on woodcock, two for two on grouse that day—limiting out on both species.

In going through the swamp I had to be concerned about myself and getting through, so I couldn't concentrate too much on the whereabouts of the dog. Consequently, she worked off her initial edge. I've heard old timers used to do this by turning their canine charges loose at the vehicle, then sitting down and leisurely smoking a pipe full of tobacco while their upland charges roamed aimlessly.

One or two scoldings after I made the swamp exit and got close to the aspen hotspot brought her in plenty close. She seemed to sense that the fun was over, she hadn't smelled a thing of interest in the swamp. The aspen ahead must have looked as promising and exciting to her as it did to me.

She made point after point, rock steady in reliability, fetched every bird, including one that took a long search before she sniffed it out. When five birds graced the game pocket in the back of my coat, I was willing to take on that swamp again.

Two grouse in the afternoon, one over Star, the other over Honey, my lab, put the perfect icing on that day. I've been carrying that 20-gauge Franchi a lot since.

Are woodcock becoming more wary? Are they flushing a little wilder, running a littler more than they once did? I think so. There are still plenty of tims that sit tight as a tick on a thick-haired setter, but these birds are becoming a little more wary every season. No wonder. More and more wingshooting enthusiasts are pursuing them, so it's survival of the fittest.

Star points dead. She was trained this way because of her hard mouth.

However, I don't think a change in dog tactics is warranted. I did suggest that today's grouse dogs should be closer working canines than they were even a decade ago. Wide ranging dogs tend to flush more grouse—simply because those wary grouse are so touchy these days. But I'm already recommending reasonably close workers for woodcock. My point is only that the hunter needs to be more aware of this new tim characteristic and not always blame his dog for unproductive points (a polite term for false pointing), birds that go airborne as the dog skids to a stop, etc. Although flushers can do as well on woodcock as they do on grouse, I hate to see a bird that sits as tight as a woodcock spoiled by the lack of a stalwart point. Of course, if these birds continue to get more jittery with increased hunting pressure, pointing dogs that can handle them might become fewer and farther between.

As recommended for grouse, flushers like goldens, labs and, springers should be given the rudiments of retrieving with pigeons. Other than that, little additional training is required. Put such dogs down in cover with birds and they'll learn the rest on their own.

A woodcock covert can hold a lot of birds in a relatively small span of space. Conversely, there are usually only a few grouse in an expansive covert. This is my main reason for recommending woodcock dogs that are much closer than grouse dogs —otherwise they pass up too much game.

A physical problem with hunting dogs has surfaced in recent years. Perhaps it was always prevalent and today's increased communications only make the problem seem more apparent. It centers around bird dogs and hounds taking fits. It has occurred with only two dogs I've owned, but I've talked with several others who have encountered the same situation. Invariably it occurs with the best of hard-driving dogs. I've never heard of it happening to a potlicker with no fire and desire.

My dogs' fits can be easily described. The dogs seem to run totally out of gas. They start trembling all over, and their pupils dilate appreciably. Soon they appear blind, their staggering walk takes them into vegetation, indicating their eyes must be totally out of focus. Ultimately they can't go any farther. After ten or twenty minutes they stop trembling, but they're so physically spent after that (and their owners are so scared) that it's the end of the hunting for that day.

On a recent rabbit hunt in southcentral Tennessee, I talked with Theo Jones about this problem, which he had been encountering with his best beagle. His veterinarian asked that he bring the dog immediately to him the next time his beagle took a fit. The vet suspected low blood sugar. I have long suspected that some dogs simply run themselves so hard that they drain their blood of energy-producing sugar. But this was the first time I had ever heard it confirmed. That beagle's blood sugar

Author takes woodcock from his yellow lab.

Scott Harrison with a brace of woodcock and one of his pointers.

was so low that the vet couldn't understand how he was still living.

The vet recommended a dish of milk and sugar prior to every hunt. It might also be a good idea to carry a chocolate bar in your pocket. After an hour's hard running the dog will probably inhale it. The dog may or may not be able to eat the candy bar after one of these fits start.

Remember, a woodcock dog is not a rare item, but that fact doesn't make the thrill of a point or the fetch of a downed bird any less rewarding. Woodcock can provide countless thrills —even for gunners who possess only average canines. My feet are on the ground solidly enough to realize that's what I have —average bird dogs.

9

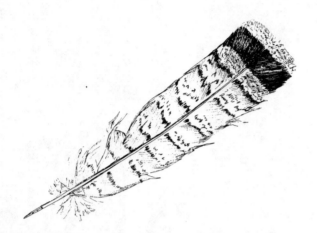

Grouse Gunnery

It was the last day of the season. I had been tramping one of the steepest grouse cover in western Pennsylvania, for that's the type of terrain birds seek when pressured by too many hunters. It hadn't been a good day for flushing ruffs, even though I had been working hard and long.

Late in the overcast, dreary afternoon, as I was wearily working my way back toward my pickup, the dog and I came across a patch of abandoned Christmas trees. They were only a few years too tall for commercial use, but they were too thick to hunt. The branches from each tree were growing into their neighbors. I skirted an outside edge strewn with red dogwood trees and grey dogwood bushes. There was plenty of fruit on both. The pines were on my left. A weed field was on my right. In the corner of the pines Magic's tinkling bell came to a halt.

There was no sense entering the evergreens. I wouldn't

have had any chance for a shot. After a brief pause to think it over I said, "All right," and the ruff roared from a ground perch. The grouse didn't make an exit my way to cross the weed field where I would have had an open shot. From the drum of its beating wings it sounded like the bird was cutting diagonally across that square of pines, but, at the time, I didn't think much about reflushing that one.

When I came to the end of the pines the bell went silent again. That's when I decided Magic had found that same bird a second time. I made two lefts to square out the pine's corners, and heard the faintest tinkle of the bell once, which permitted me to zero in on the dog's exact location.

The pines were still too thick to enter. I silently walked to where I thought I'd be in the best position. "All right," I spoke softly. That was all the impetus the grouse needed to startle into flight and head my way, too.

The bird's flush angle was down a steep hill, and he was at least fifteen yards up in the pines when he launched. Consequently, when it made an exit and started across the wide open weed field, it was flying as fast or faster than any bird I've ever seen—low to the ground—a veritable brown blur. On the skeet field, the direction and angle was a High House 4. I didn't swing far enough in front and shot behind, but I cheeked the stock more solidly for the second shot. The bird was a long way out.

While the first shot had been a 12-gauge Federal Trap load of 7½s in a paper case, the second was a long-range duck load I'd been experimenting with—the Winchester Super X Double X 1½-ounce Magnum—number 6 shot. When those big pellets struck, feathers went flying, and at the same instant the bird stuck his wings straight out and back peddled. A split second later it plummeted to the ground like a spent rocket.

I hurried to the fall area when Magic didn't find the bird on her first pass. We found it about the same time. I picked the bird from her mouth, smoothed it's feathers, patted the dog's head, and turned to look back up the steep hill. I couldn't believe how far away it was.

As soon as the bird was field dressed, I paced it off. I knew right where to go because I had been standing at the edge of the pines. It was fifty-seven long paces. That's the longest shot I've ever made on a grouse. It may have gone up to ten yards after being hit, but no farther. Actually, the memory picture I have of that indelible instant is that the bird came straight down.

I know enough about shotgun patterns at long range to know that I can't depend on killing grouse, shot after shot, at fifty-seven paces—especially with the improved cylinder choke I was using. It was a once in a lifetime grouse shot that proved the exception to the rule range wise. Fate had me outfitted with that long-range Double X load, or I'd never have bagged that bird.

In the early grouse going I usually opt for my 20-gauge Franchi 48/AL. At five pounds it carries like a feather. I can hunt with it for five or six hours, over the toughest terrain imaginable, and my arms are not fatigued.

Later in the year, when leaves are down and there are numerous hunters afield, grouse can become more wary. They tend to flush at greater average distances. They've grown their winter feathers, so they're a little more downy, making it tougher for pellets to penetrate. I find that grouse are often more pressured late in the season if other small game populations are down—like rabbits, ringnecks, squirrels, etc. Sports who normally hunt these critters will often turn to grouse if there's little else to pursue.

That's when I sometimes switch to the 12-gauge. I like a grouse gun that's light, but no 12 handles like the Franchi 20. My choice is the Franchi 12. Mine weighs six pounds, four ounces. Stock dimensions are exactly the same as the 20-gauge —fourteen-inch length of pull, 1½-inch drop at comb, and 2¼-inch drop at heel. Except for weight, I'm essentially shouldering the same gun—no matter which Franchi I opt for.

There's no question that the Franchi 12 doesn't carry as easily as the 20. I can hunt two hours with the 12 without fatigue in tough terrain, but after that my arms start to feel

The port arms carry with the Franchi 12. This ready-carry position is necessary when shooting grouse.

the extra weight. I'm positive I can't get on target quite as fast, but I know I'm still fast with this 12.

What that 12 loses to the 20 in fast handling, it gains in more pellets on the target and in one degree of choke. My 20 sports a cut off twenty-three-inch barrel with no choke. The 12 tube measures twenty-four inches—choked improved cylinder by the factory.

All three of the biggest ammunition manufacturers, Federal, Remington, and Winchester, market excellent fodder for trap enthusiasts. The most important advantage this ammo gives the hunter is the pellets—composed of extra hard shot. These pellets break targets better, penetrate into bird's flesh farther, break wing bones easier, and, perhaps most importantly, pattern with more density since the hard pellets don't deform during the trauma of powder ignition or their flight down the barrel.

In close range shooting, deformed pellets, which often fly out of the shot pattern, are an advantage. However, when grouse are particularly wild, I find the trap loads (I like 7½s or 8s best) provide exactly the right combination of pattern density and deep penetration. These loads actually pattern better (usually far better) than the so-called "High Brass" loads for which we pay more. Some say the ammunition manufacturers sell their hard pellet trap stuff at less profit because they're after the prestige of being a part of winning important clay bird championships.

My choice of the Super X Double X Magnum for my second shot in late season when grouse are wary is wrong, but I'm going to continue to pack this load in the magazine for awhile. These loads have amazed me on numerous occasions when I have been after ducks, geese, squirrels, and turkeys. One thing is absolutely certain: firing them in a six-pound, four-ounce shotgun does tend to jar the fillings, bruise the shoulder, open the eyes, and cause a few head shakes. But how many times is the second shot loosed by experienced grouse hunters? Certainly the average would be only a few per day. It's not like being on a trap or skeet field where one has to take the punishment repeatedly.

Though I move up in gun during late hunting if grouse are consistently jumping wild, I end up carrying my super light 20 most of the season. This is the medicine that brings down grouse over the long haul—the type of shotgun more ruff buffs should be carrying.

While I've carried at least two score of different upland guns in the last decade and a half, I keep going back to my 20-gauge Franchi 48/AL. When people pick this one up, they can't believe it. A common comment is, "There's nothing to it." I remember the first time I ever shouldered mine. It was at the famous gun store, Flaig's, situated in a Pittsburgh suburb. I was there having one of my shotguns repaired. While waiting I picked up most of the guns they had racked. When I picked up the Franchi and nestled it against my shoulder the first time, I knew it was mine. A week later I put a scoped 243 Winchester with double set triggers up for trade, paid the extra money willingly, and took the Franchi home.

At that time it was a twenty-six-inch bored I.C. I did well with it the first season, but when it was over I determined to shorten the barrel, which would make it even handier and would remove the choke. The gunsmith scoffed at my idea of putting his saw to work on this already light muzzle, but at my insistence he hacked. The next fall I kept track. It was the greatest grouse shooting year I had ever experienced; I shot a phenomenal 78 percent. That year was a fluke because I've never come close to that average since, but you'll never convince me that having the right shotgun wasn't the prime factor in my vast improvement.

That year there were lots of grouse and plenty of other small game critters, so the birds were never overly spooky. Short range shots were consistently the order of the day. That same year I paced off the yardage from where I had taken the shot to where I picked up the bird. I killed thirty-three grouse that year (Pennsylvania's limit is only two per day). The average bird was picked up only twenty-three yards from where I had shot.

The yardage is typical—at least that's what I've found over the years. So for normal grouse gunning who needs any choke whatever, or who needs more than an ounce of shot? Put the pattern where the grouse is, and you'll kill him.

There's more to consistently killing grouse than one ounce of shot fired from an open tube. I'm convinced that one of the most important keys is having the shotgun ready to bring into play instantly. Standard weight shotguns simply weigh too much for present day Americans to carry at the port arms position all day long. Actually, it's difficult to carry the five-pound Franchi at the port arms for hours on end without changing the carry from time to time. But the mental toughness to carry a grouse gun continually ready to bring to the shoulder can be mastered—if a super light is chosen.

Light weight is important once the swing starts, too. On the skeet field I prefer a heavy shotgun, one that absorbs recoil and one that stays ahead of the target while I'm getting the right sustained lead. Then a heavy muzzle tends to continue to swing when I pull the trigger. But while I'm taking the time to sustain my lead on a High 4 target, a grouse has vanished behind foilage or beyond the thicket.

A whippy, muzzle-light shotgun gets to the target while the average skeet gun is still being hiked toward the shoulder. The tendency with a muzzle-light gun is to over-swing, but when it comes to fast grouse shooting, I'll take all the over-swing I can get. That's exactly what I need if the shot string is to connect with the fast-departing ball of feathers.

While a shorter-than-normal barrel increases the muzzle lightness I like for this type of shooting, one of these tinier tubes is also more welcome in the thicket where brown birds are in residence. A twenty-three-inch barrel will simply hang in limbs far less frequently than a twenty-six-inch tube.

The Franchi 20 isn't the only top grouse gun considera-tion. Ithaca has a special version of their renowned Model 37 pump—their Ultrafeatherlight. This one is a 20 with vent rib and twenty-five-inch I.C. barrel. It has weight shaved in a number of ways, but the end result is a five-pound gun that comes to the shoulder like greased lightning and gets the shot headed toward the target faster than most any smoothbore on the market. There are many who enjoy shooting the chuck-

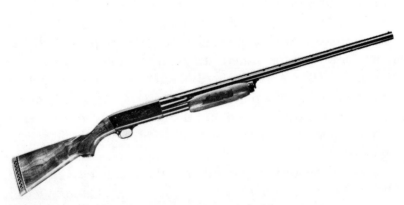

The lightweight Ithaca 20-gauge, a five-pound gun.

em-out action. Grouse trampers in this category would do well to pay the money required of this one. It's a very specialized piece of upland ordnance, and, if past history is any rule to judge by, Ithaca will produce them for a few years, sales won't meet expectations, and the model will be discontinued. A year or more later, thousands will find it a perfectly outstanding upland piece, every one who has ever heard a grouse flush will want one, and they'll become collector's items. Get one now—while they're still cheap.

My super light 20s might not be for every grouse buff. Although I stand at six feet, two inches and weigh 200 pounds, I don't dig coal, carry heavy loads like a stevedore, manhandle heavy machinery, or otherwise develop my biceps to bring in bread. Those who do might be able to handle grouse guns that weigh more than five pounds—and handle them effectively. There are other choices.

Certain over/under types are good choices. A top consideration is SKB's model 600 or the English version, the 680. The 20-gauge in either totes at six pounds, four ounces (with some a little less, depending on wood density). The quality of this model is outstanding, one of the best dollar values on the market. The 600 comes in a skeet and skeet choking. The most open available in the English-style 680 is I.C. and modified.

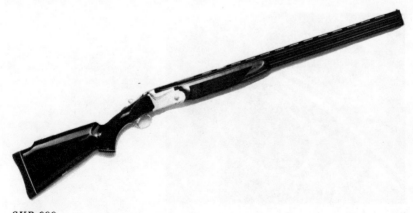

SKB 600.

SKB 600 pistol-grip checkering.

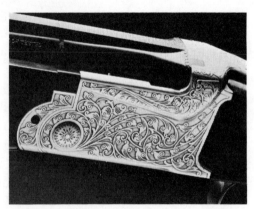

SKB 600 with outstanding receiver etching.

SKB Safety.

Another favorite is the Winchester 101 Pigeon grade. At 6½ pounds, the 20-gauge is a dandy. Like the SKB 600, the receiver is not blued but silver. The field model is fast handling and light, but there is a skeet version that weighs the same.

Winchester 101 Pigeon grade.

Browning's Citori gets excellent marks, too. For the grouse buff who can carry a little more weight than what I call the super lights, their Sporter model in 20-gauge weighs six pounds eleven ounces, according to their catalog. It features a straight grip and Schnabel-type fore-end. I have a straight grip on a custom 20 side-by-side and like it. It feels more comfortable for carrying. I have not, as yet, trimmed away the pistol grip from my downy-light Franchi. Because of the different angle the right hand takes during shouldering, the straight grip tends to make the shooter cheek the stock a little more. This is good because most shooters may not cheek the stock at all when an extra fast shot presents itself. The result is invariably a miss.

I've tried the new Ruger Red Label over/under. The one I shot was one of their earlier models. It weighed over seven

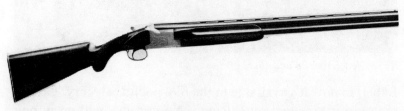

Browning Citori Sporter with Schnabel fore-end and English straight grip.

pounds, which is fine for work on doves, but too heavy once the thicket is entered. I'm told that the Ruger engineers have been back to the drawing board to trim ounces from the Red

Ruger Red Label 20 and three grouse.

Label, so now it's available in the 6½-pound category. Crafts-
manship is excellent on this one. No gun nut will go wrong
adding the Red Label to his weapon's base.

In the side-by-side line of light upland ordnance we can
again look at the SKB's. Their model 200 and English 280 are
tops. Earlier in my career I liked the side-by-sides best (and the

pumps), but as time has given me more experience I've come to prefer the single sighting plane. Now I usually opt for the over/unders (or, in the case of my grouse and woodcock pursuits, the 20-gauge Franchi). But a balanced side-by-side is a treasure to behold, and the little SKB's are certain to increase in value as time goes on.

The Bernardelli Elio Model is perhaps the best selection for the side-by-side fancier who wants to throw wide patterns and 1⅛-ounce loads. In 12-gauge this one is a magical six pounds, one ounce. The Franchi 451 Perigrine over/under 12 weighed the same, but it did not enjoy much sales success and was discontinued. To try to find one at a decent price now would be like trying to find a bargain priced Browning Superposed, which was also discontinued—not because of drooping sales, but because of tremendously escalating price.

In autoloaders, the time tested Remington 20-gauge Lightweight 1100 must receive some of the best marks. Toting at five pounds, twelve ounces, it is a joy to shoot. The new Ithaca

Remington 1100 20-gauge lightweight.

pump has already been covered—their new Ultrafeatherlight 20. The Remington 870 pump, in 20-gauge, comes close to the super lights, weighing only about eight ounces more at 5½ pounds. This chapter has not covered all the lightweights, but is intended to give the reader a range of alternatives.

Once the grouse gun has been properly selected, before going afield, the grouse buff should choose the best possible

Remington 870 lightweight pump.

loads for the work ahead. I've already mentioned the rather odd ball-fodder I stuffed in my 12-gauge Franchi for wary grouse in late season. Under normal hunting conditions I carry the 20 loaded with different stuff.

Though I carry an autoloader capable of holding two shells in the magazine, I only carry one. Why tote extra ounces between my hands all season if I'm not going to use them? Once every few years I encounter the situation where a third shell may have been useful, but I prefer to carry that extra shell in a pocket—not between my hands.

The first shell I shoot at grouse, the one in the chamber, is usually a one-ounce load of 8s—the soft shot that almost all reloaders buy. In an open boring, it spreads quickly, providing the widest possible pattern at normal grouse ranges—which are very close. I fire the second shot at only 25 percent of the birds. Some grouse are killed on the first shot, many are simply gone from sight as I pull the trigger the first time, or they disappear before I can react again. For a little added insurance on a possible second shot I opt for Federal's Premium loads in 20-gauge one ounce of 8s. This is hard shot, copper-plated so it patterns tighter than softer shot, and it will penetrate a little farther into the escaping bird's flesh, especially if the distance is a little greater, as it always is by the time the second shot is loosed.

I use Federal Premiums in a lot of other hunting situations, too. It will be a sad day when Federal decides they can no longer afford to produce and advertise shotgun shells that don't sell well. In case that happens with the Premiums, I'm going out this afternoon and order a case of 20-gauge one ounce 8s. For second shots that should last me through the last grouse I ever flush. If you ever find anything you like, buy a lifetime supply, because that product might soon be discontinued.

Every grouse hunter I've ever questioned can vividly remember the first grouse he ever killed. Many years ago I was gunning cottontails with two friends. We had a beagle pack to ring the woods with music. At that time I don't think I'd ever fired a shot at a grouse. They were too fast, they scared me too much, all around they were simply too tough.

But we flushed four or five birds in a group that afternoon as we worked up through a thick grape tangle searching for rabbit sign. We watched each grouse roar out of that tangle and zoom into a patch of tall pines to our right. I suggested we alter our course and give those grouse a reflush try—why I don't know—for we had never followed them up before.

Several flushed out while we were in those pines, but, as is typical for this type of cover, they were out of sight before any of us could shoulder a shotgun. When we got to the end of the pines a grouse flushed no more than ten feet to my left, furiously beating its wings, trying to make an uphill escape. I slammed my rabbit ordnance to my shoulder and stood there wide-eyed in surprise as the bird came skittering to the ground, still beating its wings like a drummer, but obviously dying.

I charged over, picked up the bird while his heart and wings were drumming their last, throat choked with emotion, and have been a grouse addict since that moment.

What about that gun? Even on my first grouse ever it was well suited to the task—an Ithaca Model 37—their famous pump gun that is feather light. This one was a 16-gauge, and I had the Poly-Choke Company saw back the barrel and add their adjustable choking device. It was twenty-five inches in length, and the day I killed that first grouse I had the choke wound open as far as it would go. I had found that I simply killed more rabbits with it adjusted that way.

In the years that followed, the 16-gauge pump eventually found its way to the trading block. I can't remember now which shotgun I acquired to replace it, but that doesn't matter. Perhaps I would have been better off to keep that little light pump to this day. Sometimes I wonder about changing guns too often. There is reason to believe it louses up good work in the woodlands. But the nature of the outdoor writing business is to keep doing and trying new things.

10

Woodcock Weaponry

There are several areas in northwestern Pennsylvania that I depend on every October to consistently produce birds. Two of my favorites are often so full of timberdoodles I can sometimes catch their dank odor myself. I was plowing a portion of one of those thickets last season, and skeet champion Rich Drury was my hunting partner that day. We had bagged some birds early in the morning, but the second patch was covered with splatter and the air filled with twittering wings.

On the first find my old campaigner, Star, and Rich's shorthair, Bridget, combined on a double point. I had the open shot as Rich walked in, but never fired because Drury toppled the 'doodle before it made its exit from the thick cover where he and the dogs were. From that spot we worked down off a low ridge into a bowl shaped thicket that promised briar scratches, limb whips, thorn punctures, and birds. It reeked of woodcock. It's in a place like this where my diminutive Franchi 48/AL 20-gauge shines.

Rich had pocketed his fourth bird over the two-dog point referred to last paragraph, so he only needed one more to fill his limit. I was behind with only two birds in the bag. One of the dogs was working ahead as we battled our way down the sloping bank into the bowl which turned out to be a veritable

Author with limit of timberdoodles, bird gun, and yellow lab.

amphitheater of woodcock. We heard the feather finder flush a bird, its wings twittering through the patch. Then a second bird went out, followed by a third jinking in another direction. We could only hear them though. Rich stayed on the periphery. He didn't have to catch up like I did.

It was a jungle, but birds kept bursting. The dogs were drunk. There was no controlling them, but I did my share of chastising. Finally Star had one nailed close by. I could see her four spindly legs as I bent over on my hands and knees. Her head was arched low to the ground with that extra intent look in her eye—the attitude she always displayed when there was a timberdoodle in front.

It seemed there was no way to get to her, no opening I could second guess the bird to fly toward, nothing to do but keep forging ahead, hoping some type of shot would present itself. When the bird made its exit, I caught one glimpse of long beak and brown blur. Somehow I got the Franchi, which I had been carrying in my right hand by the pistol grip, to my shoulder and snapped off a shot. I felt like the bird was covered and thought I caught a glimpse of the critter folding.

I forged ahead with new vigor. I was literally on my knees trying to get to that bird and I couldn't even remember if I had taken time to reload. Then another woodcock launched—a half-invisible gnome. It was only scant yards away as I slammed the Franchi to my shoulder and fired. Leaves and limbs flew as the shot tried to make its way to the target. Somehow I saw that one connect. Star went to that fall immediately, and I spent ten minutes trying to no avail to find the bird I had shot at first. In the meantime the dogs were ranging from one end of the little bowl to the other and flushing birds with their drunken antics. I assumed I missed that first bird, but that was easy to do with so many other woodcock there.

I worked out toward the periphery of the thicket where Rich was still trying to call his dog in and gain some degree of control over her. I did the same with mine, but as Star came in close she locked on point—under thick crabs. How would I get this one to flush?

I walked in as far as I could go and the woodcock made an exit out the opposite side. Helplessly I listened as wings twittered but I couldn't see the quarry. As the bird appeared for a second in an opening, I slammed a load of 8s toward that skylined circle. Bird number four came down. While Star and I were trying to pick that one up, Bridget pointed in front of Rich and the tim flew across the only opening in the bowl. He missed with both his 28-gauge barrels, tubes which Simmons had fitted to his 20-gauge Browning Superposed. Rich was still swearing when we reconnoitered and planned how to hunt this patch next. We both knew we'd each soon have one more bird that would fill our limit of five each.

Drury sacked his last as we worked down through a patch of higher crabs that bordered the north side of the bowl. I followed my dog down through a creek bottom, for she appeared to be working a runner. She pointed on one side of the creek, but I couldn't flush anything. I stepped across the little run and the bird came helicoptering up. When it jinked to the south, I loosed my first load, then a second. But the tim kept flying, though one leg was hanging straight down indicating a hit. Star pointed that one on the follow-up. When I was about ten yards away I saw the 'doodle lying on the ground in front of her. There wasn't a quiver of life left. We had both limited out. Five birds had fallen to our light, fast-handling guns in that cover. The whole exercise had taken less than twenty minutes. Woodcock hunting isn't like that often, but when it is, the thrills are worth waiting for.

The main point I want to make with that little interlude of hunting action is that most any but a five-pound gun would have saddled my efforts in that almost impossible tangle. I spent half the time carrying the Franchi with one hand while I was in the thicket. I can carry a 6½-pound gun like this for only short periods. Additionally, two of my three shots had to strike as fast as a cobra. The muzzle-light, short-barreled gun permitted me to get a shot off, and in the target area, whereas I doubt that I'd have been able to react in time, or get to the target area with a standard-weight upland piece.

By now readers might think I've been bought out by Stoeger Arms, the guys who import Franchis from Italy. Though I have received a number of test guns from various manufacturers over the years, I bought the 20-gauge Franchi back in 1965, before I ever entered the outdoor writing field. What makes this woodcock ordnance effective is downright simple— its minimal weight and muzzle lightness.

Today the Franchi is no longer the only five-pound smooth-bore on the market. Ithaca has entered the picture with a special version of its time tested Model 37 pump. I have not put this bottom ejector through any tests yet, but I plan to. Outfitted with a twenty-five-inch barrel and I. C. choke, it should be very effective. Hopefully Ithaca will consider bringing this one out with no choke or a skeet choke to make it even more attractive to knowledgeable grouse and woodcock maniacs. The twenty-five-inch barrel could be trimmed back to twenty-two or twenty-three inches (check local regulations regarding barrel length), and that would eliminate most if not all the choke, while not making this already light shotgun too muzzle-light and unbalanced. This one does not come with a plain barrel—only the vent rib variety—so that makes barrel cutting more complicated. The Franchi comes with either type barrel—plus a twenty-four-inch bored true cylinder.

Extra barrels can be added to either the 37 or the Franchi. I've been thinking about adding a second 20-gauge Franchi barrel to my weaponry. I'd stay with my time tested twenty-three-inch cylinder bore barrel for woodcock and early grouse going, perhaps changing to a twenty-four-inch improved cyl-inder barrel when the woodcock had departed for warmer climes and the grouse were flushing a little wilder. This same idea could be utilized with the Ithaca pump—a sawed-off, no choke barrel for early shooting, then a twenty-five-inch I. C. for later going.

Several years ago I had a custom 20 made up for timber-doodles. The price was unbelievably low. For $218 the shot-gun buff could order his choice of 12 or 20 side-by-side—a box lock made by Mario Beschi in Italy, imported by a California firm called J-K Imports. I have not had any reply to correspondence I've sent them in recent years, so they may no longer be in business. The political problems in Italy may have caused their demise.

For that unexplainably low price one could order his choice of barrel length, chokes, complete stock dimensions (making it truly a custom smoothbore); and there was a choice of three different fore-ends, three different grips, even a choice of checkered butt—all at no extra charge. For only twenty dollars one could order select walnut, too, which I did.

My order went in for a 20-gauge with twenty-four-inch barrels choked true cylinder and improved—specialized woodcock weaponry. I also opted for a splinter fore-end and straight grip. At the time I figured I shot better with more drop in the stock (why I don't know), so that's the way this custom job was ordered. A few years ago in Michigan, after spending many summer hours on the skeet field and learning to cheek a shotgun well, I found I couldn't hit the Gladwin County grouse and woodcock. I was simply bringing the stock to my cheek correctly, so the shotgun no longer fit the way it did when I

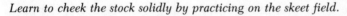

Learn to cheek the stock solidly by practicing on the skeet field.

fired with the piece away from my cheek or hardly touching. The result in Michigan was miss after miss. I should have had the little double made with the same dimensions as my Franchi, which had always been a gun that produced a high percentage of kills for me.

The saddest part of this gun story is that these light custom guns are, evidently, no longer available. Even if they were, the price would undoubtedly be sky-high compared to the pittance I paid in the early seventies.

This brings up the question—is it worth being custom fitted for a shotgun? My answer is no, perhaps a little startling to many shotgunners. I've watched others fit shooters on occasion, and here's what happens. In each case the gunner had relatively little shooting experience. He was given an adjustable try gun and asked to fire at a target that had just been painted with white lead. It was readily apparent where his shot pattern hit, so the instructor would make a few adjustments to the try gun and soon have the gunner hitting the middle of the target area.

If a gunner has tens of thousands of rounds of experience at shotgunning, then exact gun fitting becomes a plausible route. But the inexperienced gunner will almost always have rather poor shooting habits. While he may be fitted as a novice to hit the target area, in time he's going to develop proper habits —like putting the stock in the pocket of his shoulder rather

"Try gun" stock by Reinhart Fagen, stockmakers in Warsaw, Missouri. This adjustable stock is used to custom fit each individual shooter.

than out on his arm, cheeking the stock the same way every shot, his hand may move in or out on the fore-end until he finds the right place for him, he may adjust his trigger grip hand slightly—which always changes how the gun feels against the cheek. There are other shooting habits that will change and improve with time, too. In the interim the tyro shotgunner has paid a lot for a fine customized shotgun that no longer fits.

The more practical financial route is to experiment in a store with many guns to find which ones come close to fitting well. Throw up a multitude of smoothbores to find out, then check that company's catalog to find their exact stock dimensions. Next trim the stock on your current woodcock piece to those dimensions, or opt for a new super light with those dimensions. What fits the average shooter in this country is a stock of 14 to 14½ inches in length of pull, 1½-inch drop at the comb, and 2¼ to 2½-inch drop at heel. (See illustration.) Most shooters will be able to adjust to these measurements with experience. Many require a little cast-off in the stock so the rib is aligned properly (resulting in a shot that goes to the target area and not slightly to one side). Many gunsmiths can put ⅛-inch cast-off in a stock by bending it over steam, assuming there are no wood flaws in the grip area.

Once your woodcock or grouse gun fits fairly well, it's time to practice. Do it at home and always check that the gun is empty when you pull it from the pegs. Throw it up often. After it's up, focus your eyes in close, on the barrel or rib. Is it

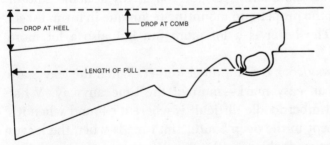

Critical measurements for fitting a gun are drop at heel, drop at comb, and length of pull.

lined up straight? Are you seeing too much rib? Or too little? Keep working at throwing the gun up and getting the perfect barrel/rib picture. Learn what it feels like when it's perfect. Only repetitive practice can accomplish this, but you can get that repetition if you pull your upland gun off the pegs every day. Pull it to your shoulder four or five times each day—that's all it takes.

On the skeet field, when I shoulder a skeet gun I first look down the rib to make certain I have the perfect picture—the two beads are seen as a figure eight and the rib is aligned straight. Most shooters prefer not to look at the rib, focusing only at a distance where the target will be. Once I'm certain my rib and beads are aligned perfectly, and that my gun is shouldered properly, I refocus my eyes to the target area, then come back to the house, taking an extra second or two to make certain my eyes are distance-focused before I call for the target.

This technique has definitely helped me in game cover. Because I shoot a lot of skeet I'm aware of proper gun mounting in the hunting field. The result is that I naturally shoulder the shotgun in woodcock cover the right way because I'm so familiar with the way it should feel. I've had numerous pictures taken of me lately, with the photo snapped just as I pulled the trigger, and I consistently have the gun cheeked. Years ago I often fired when the butt was too low on my shoulder and the stock wasn't touching my cheek. I'm positive this is a problem many other shooters encounter. The way to cure the dilemma is by shouldering the gun repeatedly at home, and/or working at the proper gun mounting technique in formal skeet shooting. The latter is a lot more fun but also a lot more expensive.

The woodcock is not a tough target. When the leaves are down, it's an easy mark—most of the time anyway. What makes the timberdoodle difficult is where it's found when it's found. Except in the deep South, tim time is when the leaves have set the woods ablaze with color. When the leaves go down, most woodcock are basking in sunny warmth a lot farther

Author works woodcock cover with Ruger Red Label 20-gauge.

south than my bailiwick. The fall foliage gunner finds woodcock an exhilarating challenge because grouse can be completely impossible at that time of year. So many of them flush
and are never seen. But the aspen or alder tramper gets more
than the occasional glimpse of woodcock as he forges the thick
cover, and quick shots with the barrels hanging in thin limbs
are what this gunning is all about.

I'm convinced that any degree choke in a woodcock piece
gives the bird an added chance to escape, and the bird already
has a lot in its favor. Few gun companies offer cylinder-bore
guns, and I can't figure out why. Grouse and quail pursuers
should jump on them as soon as they reach the gun store shelves.
But woodcock are consistently shot closer than any other game
bird, and the no-choke gun pays off in more birds.

Maybe the sawed-off tube is the answer (check local regulations), for this is the way to get a close range piece that has a

true cylinder bore. At the same time one can also trim muzzle weight a bit. This results in a balance that swings quicker to a target that usually presents itself for only the shortest time.

For shells, I like 8s or 9s when I'm on woodcock tramps. I usually stuff the chamber with a skeet reload, then follow it up with a factory shell in the magazine. I refuse to carry the extra weight of the third shell between my hands all season long. I can depend on the factory fodder chambering properly in my autoloader. My reloads are slightly less reliable. The second shot is fired a relatively small percentage of the time, so a box of factories might last most of the season.

While I sometimes like the insurance of the Federal Premium one-ounce load of 8s for the back up, I usually carry the standard $7/8$-ounce stuff, always a $7/8$-ounce load in the chamber. Woodcock are among the easiest birds in the uplands to kill, and the range is always short. The energy from a pellet or two is still high at ten yards—usually enough to do the job. The main thing in upland shooting is to put the center of the shot pattern in the vicinity of the target. There's no more telling secret to success in October than that one premise. The right gun goes a long way toward permitting any gunner to consistently accomplish that task.

11

Attire and Gear

The wrong boots will soon have the grouse or woodcock hunter leg-weary, and he won't be able to hunt as far. The wrong pants won't provide needed briar protection, and he won't be able to get in where the birds are. With the wrong shirt or coat, perspiration will soak the hard-working hunter, effectively cutting back his enthusiasm while unnecessarily increasing his metabolism. With the wrong hat, he spends too much time catching his fedora as it falls, or bending over picking it up, often at the precise moment the quarry decides to lift from its launch pad.

As a grouse and woodcock hunter gains more experience with each passing season, he tends to become enamored with specific equipment he favors. Often these opinionated feelings are arrived at because what he has come to approve is so much better than the gear he previously used for that purpose. How-

The L. L. Bean rubber bottom/leather top pac is lightweight and ideal for many upland hunting forays.

ever, there may be another type of gear that he hasn't tried yet which might be even better. The point is that the quest for better and more efficient outdoor gear goes on. The manufacturers come up with better and better products, so the best attire and equipment change from time to time.

One favorite item that fails to be improved upon, as far as grouse and woodcock hunting are concerned, is the L. L. Bean rubber bottom/leather top pac, commonly known as the Maine Hunting Shoe. This is a boot I wear for more and more purposes with every passing season. There are several reasons for their success and continued use. Weight is of course the primary consideration for the hunter who travels over a lot of country in a day. The ten-inch pac (the height I favor) in size 9EE weighs a token two pounds, fourteen ounces. It's doubtful any boot weighs less. Certainly there are none that offer this boot's utility in that weight class.

But heft is only one criteria for this boot being so well suited to grousing and woodcocking. The sole design is also of critical importance. Its chain pattern and reasonably soft rubber mean the wearer can feel the ground through these boots.

The result is less tripping and stumbling, because hazards on the ground are felt before they can trip the hunter. Not all are aware of this feature, for it's subtle, not easily appreciated.

On the other hand, the somewhat soft sole is a liability when hunting extremely rocky ground for long periods of time. In steep terrain the chain tread does not give the best gripping surface. When either of these conditions are encountered, I still opt for the L. L. Bean pacs, but I switch to the Vibram Soled Maine Hunting Shoe. These are heavier; a 9C weighs three pounds, eight ounces. The vibram sole used in conjunction with these boots is reasonably soft. The boots come only in the 9-inch height, and expense is approximately 25 percent greater.

The cost of the standard Maine Hunting Shoe is a definite plus. With many quality outdoor boots now approaching the triple figure price range, L. L. Bean has been doing a commendable job in keeping their prices down, though they too are escalating to a degree.

Once a blanket of snow covers the ground, I pull out the Bean boots with the Vibram soles, waterproofing the leather portion heavily with liquid silicone. These have heavier rubber, giving a little more warmth. Unless temperatures become extremely cold, I can stay with these for the remainder of the season. In March, when dog training gets into full swing again, I switch back to the standard Bean pacs.

New lightweight, close-weave fabrics have been a boon to the uplander. Pants made of such fabrics combine briar-turning qualities with light weight. The best of these pants are faced with some sort of extra protection. Some incorporate two layers of thickness in front and utilize the same material for both layers. Others make use of other facing materials. One of the best is a light-weight nylon, another is leather-like. The original leather-like material was extremely heavy, and in cold weather it became stiff, making walking that much more difficult. Bean offers two types of pants with the newer, leather-like fabric that stays pliable at all temperatures but still provides the ultimate in briar protection.

New lightweight hunting pants with facing which ends at the top of the thigh.

The last few years I've been attaching suspenders to my hunting pants and leaving my belt at home. It's amazing how much less fatiguing this simple change in attire can be. The advantage is that the pants can slip up and down over the knee much easier while walking. Extra energy is required to walk when a belt is used, especially stepping up over logs, blow-downs, etc. Anyone trying suspenders instead of a belt for hunting will quickly appreciate the advantages of the former.

One place where virtually every manufacturer falls down in facing their pants is that they don't bring the facing right up to the belt line. This may be a cost-saving measure, or it may be a carry-over from days when facings were stiff and non-pliable. Current pant facings end just below the body crease, where the wearer's thigh attaches to the torso. While walking, a V is created at this point, and many briars that are slipping upward on the pants or downward off the coat or vest end up in this area where there is no facing material. The result is constant thorn and briar jabs. Pants made solely of extra-heavy duck material will ward off briars and provide complete protection for this area. But duck material is much heavier, less pliable, much more difficult to walk in. What is needed is a manufacturer who will offer pants made of the new lightweight, close-weave material with a modern facing that comes all the way to the belt line.

I'm a blaze orange color advocate because of one startling statistic. No one has ever been shot in mistake of game who has been wearing this color. To increase my chances even further, I wear as much blaze orange as I can find. For a few years 10X made both vests and coats of blaze orange. These were excellent. I should have purchased a lifetime supply. As stated previously, always try and do that when you find a product you think is great, because you can depend on them discontinuing that product. 10X did!

Another favorite of mine was the L. L. Bean blaze orange shirt. Made of a heavy brush-turning cloth, this was the perfect shirt to wear on cool hunting days, in conjunction with a blaze orange vest. Anyone who couldn't see a hunter in that get up would have been legally blind.

In warm weather, and if the cover isn't impossibly briar-ridden, I prefer a common, long-sleeve sport shirt and an orange vest. So clothed, I can hunt hard and long without getting overheated. When heavy briar cover must be plowed, I'll often keep the lightweight shirt but exchange my vest for a coat, either of briar-turning duck, one of the new close-weave materials, or blaze orange, though I can't find anyone who makes the latter any more.

As temperatures go down I abandon the sport shirt for either my Bean blaze orange shirt, or one of their chamois cloth shirts, the latter being one of the most popular items in their always delightful catalog. With either of those shirts I opt for the blaze orange vest. The chamois shirt does a commendable job of warding briars from the arms. When a vest is worn, the blaze orange shirt does an even better job.

As temperatures go further down I switch to the coat, in conjunction with one of the two heavier shirts. When temperatures go below freezing, I add a lightweight, cotton turtleneck sweater underneath my shirt, but never more topside attire.

The experienced grouse and woodcock buff knows how important it is to stay cool. A hard hunter seldom faces the problem of becoming cold, while stand-around hunters are always plagued with this dilemma. Those who pursue species like white-tailed deer, squirrels, and other game, where long stints of sitting are required for best success, must always bundle up. The attire for this type of hunting will never double in the uplands. Those who try to make warm clothes work in fast-moving hunting situations will not be satisfied.

My hat for the uplands is the dumbest-looking piece of attire I've ever seen. When I have pictures taken of me I always remove my working hat, replacing it with one more suited to the camera. I use the Bean Felt Hat, but modify it with a chin strap to keep it on my head when crossing thick cover. My chin strap is what makes it look so dumb. With a hat not fastened down in some manner, too much time and energy is wasted catching it as it falls, or picking it up from the ground. Some shot opportunities are always missed while performing one of those acts.

I punch holes through both sides of the brim with an awl. Then I push a piece of rawhide up through these holes and tie a double overhand knot so the straps won't slip down through the hole. I take a ½-inch piece of ⅜-inch wood dowel and drill a hole through the middle large enough to accommodate both pieces of rawhide coming from either side of the hat brim. The piece of dowel rod slides up and down—holding tight against the chin for walking through thick cover, down for hat removal. A knot at the bottom end of the rawhide straps prevents the dowel from slipping off.

The brim of this hat helps shield my eyes from the sun, gives my neck rain protection, and is reasonably waterproof in itself. Cost is moderate. While Bean does offer this hat in scarlet for use in the uplands, I would like to see them also market this hat to uplanders in the blaze orange shade.

When hunting unknown country I wouldn't think of leaving my vehicle without taking out my compass, checking the map for how surrounding roads run, and taking a reading to make sure I'm certain I know where I am, where I'm going, and how I can get back out. When hunting territory I've hunted before I'm not so careful, often forgetting the compass on the dash of my pickup in my haste to turn the dogs loose, load the gun, and get started. But I remember it often in this latter situation, and I use it.

My reason for using a compass does not center around a fear of getting lost, though in strange country I don't want to do that. But the primary reason for relying on a compass is to prevent wasting time. When a hunter gets turned around, loses his bearings, isn't quite sure of where his path is going to take him, he becomes a much less effective hunter. Too much time is spent figuring out where he is, determining how to get back to the vehicle, while too little time is spent accomplishing what he set out to do.

If you don't wear glasses, you should. Eye protection for hunters and shooters should be legally required, like a license for drivers. It's the only sensible and safe arrangement. Scott Harrison, mentioned earlier in this book, is an orthopedic surgeon. When he finally set up shop he almost lost it all—by failing to wear protective glasses on a woodcock hunt. A limb came back and whipped his eye, seriously scratching his lens. It was only good fortune that Scott's sight came back. His eye was bandaged for two weeks. Limbs are only one source of danger while hunting and shooting. Others are obvious, so I won't discuss them.

But the hard-driving hunter wearing eye glasses gets steamy. When he does his glasses fog up. Mine always fog on the right lens first—in the upper left hand corner of that lens —right where I need to look when peering down the barrel or rib of a favorite bird gun. A number of anti-fogging solutions are on the market. Carry one with your hunting gear or in your vehicle. One that I have used most successfully is available from D-Boone Enterprises, P. O. Box 8, Highspire, PA 17043. It's an impregnated red cloth called the No Fog Magic Cloth and sells for $2. Glasses should be cleaned with this red cloth every day. It will keep lenses fog-free.

My final suggestion will be new to most hunters. My wife works with an ambulance service. As a part of her work, we need to have what is called a Scanner. This electronic marvel has room for eight radio crystals. We needed the crystals for our local police, fire, ambulance, and hospital radio bands. As an afterthought we added a crystal for the radio band of the U. S. Weather Service in Pittsburgh.

This small investment has been a boon to my hunting. Their weather report can be turned on any time. The weatherman keeps repeating himself on tape. The forecast is updated every hour or so, even more often if something major is happening. They don't stop with only the short forecast the regular AM and FM radio stations give, either. It's a much more in-depth report, sometimes lasting for five minutes before repeating and includes long-range forecasts.

Grouse are especially attuned to weather. They're most vulnerable when weather is good, sometimes impossible when weather is bad. By keeping track of the forecast I hunt in good weather more often. I plan my work around bad weather, my hunting around sunny afternoons when I know grouse will be more active.

When hunting woodcock, I plan hunts for migratory birds around the approach of major fronts coming out of the north or northwest. Though a weather crystal might be joked about as an effective piece of equipment for upland bird hunting, don't sell it short. With one installed in your home, you'll be depending upon it more and more.

Index

Page numbers in italics refer to illustrations.

Nick Sisley and Star.

ABOUT THE AUTHOR

Nick Sisley has exceptional experience hunting both grouse and woodcock in New Brunswick, Quebec, and Ontario. His stateside quests have taken him all over Pennsylvania, Ohio, Michigan, Minnesota, New York, Maine, West Virginia, and Vermont in pursuit of these two birds. He's a skilled shotgunner whether the targets are grouse, woodcock, quail, doves, waterfowl, or clay birds. He is preparing to start his own shooting school for upland game enthusiasts and has written literally scores of national and regional magazine articles relating to grouse and woodcock. His wingshooting travels have taken him all over the world.